JIMMY WHO? ★

N EXAMINATION OF PRESIDENTIAL CANDIDATE
MMY CARTER: THE MAN, HIS CAREER, HIS STANDS
N THE ISSUES

BY LESLIE WHEELER

WITH A FOREWORD BY
JAMES W. DAVIS
Dean, College of Arts and Sciences
Professor of Political Science
Western Washington State College

 Barron's
Woodbury, New York

All inquiries should be addressed to:
Barron's Educational Series, Inc.
113 Crossways Park Drive
Woodbury, New York 11797

Library of Congress Catalog Card No. 76-21680

Library of Congress Cataloging in Publication Data

Wheeler, Leslie, 1945-
  Jimmy who?: An examination of Presidential candidate Jimmy Carter.

  1. Carter, Jimmy, 1924-   I. Title.   *Qp 23 79*
F291.3.C37W47   975.8@04@0924 [B]   76-21680
ISBN 0-8120-0748-5

International Standard Book No. 0-8120-0748-4

PRINTED IN THE UNITED STATES OF AMERICA

2 3 4 5 6 7 8 9 10 11 M 9 8 7 6

To my grandfather, the late Senator Burton K. Wheeler of Montana, the man who first taught me the meaning of political courage

Contents

Acknowledgments

Thanks are due to the following copyright owners and their publishers for permission to reprint copyrighted material:

© 1976 by the New York Times Co. on portions of articles from 5/17, 5/20, 6/4, 6/6, 6/16. With CBS on portions of articles from 2/25, 3/10, 3/17, 4/7, 4/28, 5/19, 6/9. Reprinted by permission.

© 1976 by *Harper's Magazine*, March 1976. Reprinted by permission.

Reprinted by permission of the *Atlanta Journal* © 1971, © 1974, © 1976 on portions of articles from 8/26/71, 11/26/74, 2/8/76.

Reprinted by permission of the *Atlanta Constitution* © 1976, © 1974, © 1971, © 1970, © 1966 on portions of articles from 5/6/76, 7/10/74, 1/7/71, 4/16/71, 11/8/70, 11/11/70, 7/2/66.

With permission of the *Wall Street Journal* © 1976 on portions of articles from 3/25, 5/25, 6/17.

Reprinted by permission from TIME, The Weekly News magazine; Copyright Time Inc. © 1976, © 1971 on portions of articles from 5/10/76, 2/23/76, 5/31/71.

© 1975 Broadman Press from *Why Not The Best?* All rights reserved. Used by permission.

Copyright © 1976 by Newsweek, Inc. All rights reserved. Reprinted by permission.

Allen Ehrenhart and Congressional Quarterly, Inc. Copyright © 1976.

Reprinted by permission of *New York Post*. © 1976 (21 May 1976), New York Post Corporation.

Reprinted by permission of *The New Republic* © 1976, The New Republic, Inc.

© 1976 by the *Rolling Stone*, 3 June 1976.

Reprinted by permission of Newspaper Enterprise Association, © 1976 (10 February 1976).

U.S. Naval Academy Yearbook *The Lucky Bag* of 1947.

Reprinted by permission of Charles Scribner's Sons from *The Southern Strategy* by John R. Murphy and Harold Gulliver. Copyright © 1971. John R. Murphy and Harold S. Gulliver.

Courtesy of T. McN. Simpson, Associate Professor of Political Science, University of Tennessee.

© Educational Broadcasting Corporation, 1976. Reprinted by permission.

Reprinted by permission of *New York Sunday News.* © 1976 (April 1976).

Copyright © 1976, by The Atlantic Monthly Company, Boston, Mass. Reprinted with permission.

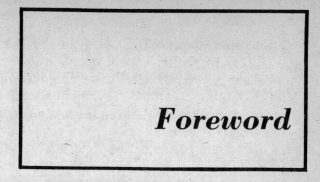

Foreword

Although the name of Jimmy Carter has recently become a household word, many American citizens are probably unaware that in October, 1975 — less than ten months before the 1976 Democratic convention — the Gallup presidential poll indicated that nationwide the former Georgia governor was the choice of only 1% of Democratic voters. Little wonder then that American voters asked "Jimmy Who?" when queried by pollsters or newsmen about the smiling Georgian. But within a period of five months Jimmy Carter jumped to second place in the Gallup poll, two points behind Senator Hubert H. Humphrey (30% to 28%); by mid-May he had forged ahead of Humphrey. Carter's meteoric rise in the polls easily surpassed presidential candidate George McGovern's record-breaking Gallup poll performance of 1972.

Following Carter's solid victory in Pennsylvania, Humphrey sensing that Carter's astonishing string of presidential primary victories over Senator Jackson, Governor Wallace, and Representative Udall had created an aura of invincibility, announced that he would not enter the 1976 race at the eleventh hour in an obvious "stop Carter" move. After "Super Bowl Tuesday" (the triple header California-Ohio-New Jersey primaries on June 8th), Carter's Democratic opponents were in complete disarray, even though Carter failed to win California and lost to an uncommitted slate in New Jersey. His 17th primary triumph in Ohio on the last day of the primary season gave Carter such a commanding lead that most of his opponents threw in their cards. Despite several setbacks in the final weeks of the campaign, Jimmy Carter had captured enough committed delegates to go over the top on the first ballot — the first Democratic nominee in the twentieth century from the out-of-power party to nail down the nomination more than a month before the convention on his first try. (Even the Grand Champ, Franklin D. Roosevelt, although he collected a majority of the delegates during the 1932 pre-convention period, did not win on the first ballot because the Democratic two-thirds rule — repealed in 1936 — required the nominee to win by a two-thirds majority. Roosevelt won on the fourth ballot.)

From the start, Democratic politicians have consistently underestimated Jimmy Carter. When democratic National Chairman Robert Strauss, in response to Carter's offer in early 1973 to help out the party in the 1974 off-year elections, appointed the Georgia governor as chairman of the Democratic National Committee's Congressional Campaign Committee, little did he realize that Carter would use the committee post as a springboard to jump into the 1976 presidential race. Throughout the 1974 Congressional campaign Carter visited over forty states, became acquainted with Congressional candidates and incumbents in most of the 435 Congressional districts across the land, and met with hundreds of state and local party officials. To handle the day-to-day duties of this job, Carter chose as his right-hand man a young 29-year-old Georgian from his governor's staff — Hamilton Jordan. This same Carter staff member emerged as Carter's national campaign manager soon after the 1974 Congressional elections that saw the Democrats capture almost two-thirds of the House of Representatives. Earlier, before the 1972 McGovern debacle, Jordan had authored Carter's master plan to capture the 1976 Democratic nomination. The Carter game plan, as reported by James T. Wooten of the *New York Times*, rested on four assumptions, which if proved correct, might open the road to the nomination — and possibly the White House:

1. That the nomination would be won in the torturous parade of over thirty primary elections and in the early-round caucus-convention states, not in the smoke-filled backrooms at the Democratic convention.

2. That fellow southerner, Governor George Wallace, despite his spectacular primary campaign in 1972 before he was gunned down by a would-be assassin, could be knocked out of the race in 1976 and his influence as a national political figure reduced to a token level.

3. That Carter's own Southern origins and his image as an unknown newcomer without ties to the Washington establishment could be turned into formidable assets, not crippling liabilities.

4. That most voters would be more favorably disposed toward a candidate stressing personal qualities — trust and integrity — than toward a candidate emphasizing his ideological stand on the issues.

Carter followed his game plan almost to the letter, entering all of the thirty-one primaries except West Virginia. Carter quickly recognized that the new Democratic party rules, adopted in 1974, guaranteed a presidential candidate a proportionate share of the delegates in most primaries. Thus, even if he did not come in first, an outsider candidate such as himself would stand a reasonable chance of picking up some delegates in almost every primary he entered. The old winner-take-all rules in several states would have made it more difficult for Carter to accumulate these batches of delegates.

Carter won seventeen out of thirty-one primary elections (no other candidate won more than four). From the opening round Iowa precinct caucuses, to the finish line in June, he accumulated sizable blocks of support in the non-primary states. By the end of the primary season on June 8th, Carter had amassed over 1,100 delegates, more than three times as many as his nearest competitor. With such an overwhelming lead, Carter neared the magic number of 1,505 delegates, the number needed to win the nomination. Carter's chief rivals, in the face of hopeless odds, conceded defeat. Less than seven days after the final three primaries in California, Ohio, and New Jersey, Carter collected an additional 400+ delegates as Governor Wallace, Mayor Richard J. Daley of Chicago, and Senator Henry "Scoop" Jackson released their delegates to him and jumped on the "Carter campaign special" before it left the station. Although a legal question arose over whether some of these pledged delegates could be released for the first ballot at the convention, no political professional — except possibly Governor Jerry Brown of California — doubted that Carter had the nomination in the bag.

Early in the primary campaign, Carter had administered a sensational one-two knockout punch to Governor Wallace in the 1976 Florida and North Carolina primaries. (Four years earlier, Wallace had lapped the field of candidates in Florida and overwhelmed Governor Terry Sanford in the North Carolina primary.) Wallace's double defeat in his home territory ended his 12-year quest of the White House although he continued to campaign perfunctorily down to the last primary. With Wallace out of the way — a key turning point in the race — Carter moved into the front-runner's spot, a lead that he never relinquished. Carter had correctly reasoned that if he could not defeat Wallace on his own turf, he would not be accepted as a viable candidate elsewhere. In demolishing Wallace, Carter chose not to take an orthodox Southern liberal traditional approach against the Alabama governor. Instead, Carter questioned Wallace's qualifications as a realistic presidential contender, suggesting repeatedly that while there was little wrong with Wallace's anti-Washington message, the Alabama governor could never become president.

Carter's giant-killer role in the early primaries, of course, focused national media attention on his whirlwind campaign. Night after night the three national television networks carried front-line stories on this political newcomer. Within a period of eight weeks "Jimmy Who?" appeared twice on the covers of both *Time* and *Newsweek*. Syndicated cartoonists had a field day with Carter's broad smile, his overstocked supply of teeth and his peanut farmer background. So preoccupied were the networks and the press with this new Southern front-runner who talked about trust and love of fellow-Americans, that they frequently ignored or overlooked his ambigious positions on the issues. When questioned, Carter refused to be pinned down specifically on the issues, stating he felt that many of them, e.g., tax reforms, were too complicated to be spelled out during the heat of the campaign. Furthermore, it was his private belief — and that of his pollster, Patrick Caddell — that issues were secondary in the mind of the average voter, who preferred a candidate exuding integrity, and confidence and promising "I will never lie to you."

As the 3,008 Democratic delegates from the fifty states and territories and the thousands of national reporters, cameramen, technicians, and visitors prepare to descend on New York's Madison Square Garden for the quadrennial extravaganza, many of them still have little first-hand knowledge about Jimmy Carter. Little more, perhaps, then countless Americans or the several million voters who cast their ballots for him in the thirty-one primaries. For that reason, Leslie Wheeler's incisive study of the first prospective Southern presidential nominee to be selected by the Democratic party in more than a century, helps fill a void in our political literature.

The reader will soon discover that the author of this compact study has drawn information from a wide variety of printed sources as well as from her own broad acquaintanceship with party professionals. A granddaughter of the late crusading Democratic Senator Burton K. Wheeler of Montana, who put aside his party label in 1924 to serve as the vice-presidential running-mate with Wisconsin Senator Robert M. "Fighting Bob" La Follette on the progressive party ticket, Ms. Wheeler furnishes the reader with many thoughtful insights about the character of the enigmatic Democratic presidential front-runner who has described himself as "a farmer, an engineer, a scientist, a politician, and a born-again Christian." Yet many baffled candidate watchers who have observed Carter demolish a dozen rival presidential aspirants within a period of 105 days still feel that they do not know who the real Jimmy Carter is. According to one party insider, "He's a conservative to conservatives, a moderate to moderates, and a liberal to liberals." While none, except possibly Carter's wife, Rosalynn, can answer definitively about who is the "real Jimmy Carter," the reader of the present study will come away with a much richer understanding of a Southern political leader who may within a few months become the 39th president of the United States.

As the nation celebrates its bicentennial and starts to move into its third century, more and more Americans are beginning to feel that it might be fitting that the country should turn to the South for its first presidential nominee since the Civil War — the nation's bloodiest conflict. (Before this war between the states, the South had been the birthplace of nine of the first fifteen presidents.) Significantly, the year 1976 also marks 100 years since the dreadful Reconstruction occupation of the South ended. Perhaps James Earl Carter, Jr., will become the president to bind up the last lingering wounds of that ill-conceived policy.

— JAMES W. DAVIS

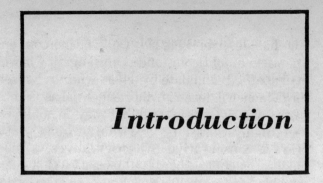

Introduction

Perhaps the most significant feature of the 1976 presidential campaign has been the emergence of former Georgia Governor Jimmy Carter from relative obscurity into the national limelight as the front-runner for the Democratic nomination. As a Southerner, a born-again Baptist, a Washington outsider, and the first statesman since George Washington to say he'll never tell a lie, Carter has aroused a tremendous amount of controversy.

His critics range from sophisticated Washington columnists to axe-wielding segregationist Lester Maddox. His supporters include people as diverse as Ann Landers and Gonzo journalist Hunter S. Thompson. He has received the endorsement of conservatives like George Wallace and liberals like Birch Bayh. He frightens some people; to others he is a great source of hope. Many, quite frankly, are puzzled by him.

"Jimmy Who?" was a question they asked in Georgia back in 1966 when Carter first ran for governor. In 1975, when Carter began his campaign for the presidency, people throughout the country also began to ask, "Jimmy Who?" Few people pose that question now because Carter is virtually assured of winning the nomination on the first ballot.

Although people now know Jimmy Carter's name, many are not familiar with his political career. "People just don't understand our Jimmy," a Georgian said recently. During Carter's four-year term as governor, Georgians had a good opportunity to observe him close at hand. The rest of the country hasn't had this opportunity and a lot of people are now trying to take a closer look at this man. What Jimmy Carter said when he ran for governor, what he accomplished in office, and how he managed to capture the presidential nomination from Wallace, Jackson, Bayh, Udall, and Humphrey may well be a key to how good a president Mr. Carter could be. Many people don't understand Jimmy, although a lot have found his views and image appealing.

This book is an attempt to shed some light on the man behind the smile and the handshake, the man who says he's going to be our next president. It does not try to be a definitive biography of the man, nor does it claim to offer scholarly discussion of the complex political makeup of this era in American politics. This book does, however, present the image of Jimmy Carter as a Southerner; it attempts to place Carter in a context of Southern politics and to deal with the forces that shaped his views as a Southerner.

I wish to acknowledge the assistance I received from so many people in researching and compiling the information for this book. In particular, I wish to thank Miss Lillian Carter, Jimmy Carter's mother, for the information she personally gave me. I also wish to thank Hal Gulliver and Bill Schipp, both of the *Atlanta Constitution,* and Jack

Spalding, of the *Atlanta Journal*. Thanks are extended to Charles Kirbo and Philip Alston, political advisers to Jimmy Carter, and extended to Ben Fortson, the secretary of state for Georgia, for the insights they offered me. I am grateful for the comments and suggestions made by James W. Davis, Dean of the College of Arts and Sciences and Professor of Political Science at Western Washington State College; by Thomas P. Murphy, Executive Director of the Institute for Urban Studies at the University of Maryland, College Park; and by Phillip Lefton, Principal of Theodore Roosevelt High School, New York City. I also wish to thank my father, John Wheeler, for the help he offered in researching the material for this book, and to thank all the people in Georgia who were so willing to talk to me about Jimmy Carter. Finally, I wish to offer my thanks for the extensive assistance I received from Barron's staff, in particular, from Carole Berglie, Evelyn Miller, Ernest Noa, and Ruth Pecan.

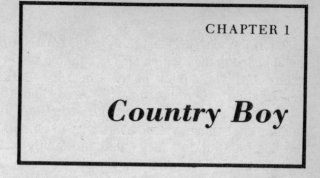

CHAPTER 1

Country Boy

South Georgia is Carter country. The first Carters came into the area around 1830, not long after the Indians had left. They were cotton farmers, merchants, and Civil War soldiers. After the war, when the slaves had gone and cotton was replaced by peanuts as the major crop, they continued as farmers, just one notch above the black sharecroppers who worked on their land.

Plains, the home seat of the Carter clan, is located in Sumter County, about twenty miles from Fort Sumter, or the infamous Andersonville, where thousands of Union soldiers died from lack of water during the Civil War. During the Civil War, Plains was a cluster of shacks at the crossing of two roads; later when the railroad came through, the town moved about a mile to snuggle next to the tracks. By the 1920s, Plains consisted of a row of storefronts; at one end was the grocery store owned by James Earl Carter, Sr.; at the other, a general store and mule auctioning center run by his brother, Alton.

James Carter and his wife, the former Lillian Gordy, lived on a farm in the rural community of Archery, three miles outside of Plains. Here on October 1, 1924, their

1

first son, James Earl Carter, Jr., was born. He grew up in a clapboard house, which lacked running water and electricity until the advent of the Rural Electrification Administration when he was 16. According to Jimmy's mother, their home was a "nice house in the country," and the fact that there was no electricity or running water in the beginning didn't mean that the family was poor. "I know Jimmy writes about how poor we were, but really, we were never poor. There was no running water or electricity but no one in the country had lights unless they built it on their own. We were just like all country people. We didn't feel poor and we always had a car. We had the first radio in Plains. We had the first TV set."[1] No, they weren't poor compared to the black families who were dependent on them for a livelihood. But they weren't rich either. The burning sun and clinging red soil of South Georgia were great equalizers, and it was only through a tremendous effort that the Carters kept themselves on a level that was slightly higher than that of the black sharecroppers.

When Jimmy was five, his mother would lift him over the fence, handing him a ladle of water to take to the workers in the fields. Later on, he joined them in the fields, getting up at 4 a.m. to the ringing of the large farm bell. He helped plow, mop cotton with a poisonous mixture to keep insects away, stack peanuts, fix fences. In his autobiography he recalls, "Our farm work was heavy all year 'round. My daddy saw to that with his widely-diversified farm industries. My school work always came first, but farm children could expect the teachers to give few time-consuming homework assignments."[2]

Jimmy worked hard because that was what his daddy

did. "In retrospect, the farm work sounds primitive and burdensome," he writes, "but at the time it was an accepted farm practice, and my dad himself was an unusually hard worker. Also, he was always my best friend."[3] He was the only son for 13 years (two sisters, Gloria and Ruth, came before his younger brother, Billy). Thus it was perhaps natural that he should have felt especially close to his father. He loved, feared, and respected his father and never even considered disobeying him — an attitude which seems to set him apart from many other young boys, then and now. As TV journalist Bill Moyers put it,"I wonder if anyone who never disobeyed his father can understand the rest of us." Jimmy's reply was this:

Well, as a matter of fact, I never disobeyed my father in that when he said — Jimmy, you do something — I failed to do it. But on many occasions I did things that I knew my father didn't like, and I was punished very severely because of it. In fact, my father very seldom gave me an order. If all the other field workers were off for the afternoon, and he wanted me to turn the potato vines so they could be plowed Monday morning, Daddy would say to me — he called me "Hot"[short for "Hot Shot"]. . . "Hot, would you like to turn the potato vines this afternoon?" And I would much rather go to the movie or something, but I always said, "Yessir, daddy, I would." And I would do it. But he didn't have to give me many direct orders, but I never did disobey a direct order . . . it wasn't a namby-pamby sort of thing. My father was my friend, and I respected him. I never said, "Yes" or "No" to my father. I'd say, "Yessir," or "No, sir." To my mother, too. Still do. And to most people I don't know well. But it was a matter of respect. It wasn't any matter of trying to cow-tow to him . . .[4]

When Jimmy did misbehave, he received a whipping. "From the time I was four years old until I was fifteen years old he whipped me six times and I've never forgotten any of those impressive experiences. The punishment was administered with a small, long, flexible peach tree switch."[5] One such whipping occurred when his father discovered that he had kept the penny he was supposed to give for the offering at church, and had also taken an additional one from the collection plate. It was the last time he ever stole money.

Earl Carter emerges as a rather stern, forbidding figure. Yet Jimmy says his father loved to have a good time and enjoyed parties more than his mother. "He laughed a lot and everybody liked him." He was not a man, however, to be laughed at. Jimmy tells the story of a time when his father bought his first tailor-made suit of clothes, and it turned out to be much too large for him. Although he must have looked ridiculous in the oversized suit, no one in the family so much as smiled.

In the white community at Plains, Earl Carter was a recognized leader. He served on the Sumter County School Board for a number of years, worked to get a new hospital, taught Sunday school at the Baptist Church, and was one of the first directors of the local Rural Electrification Administration. To the 25 black families who lived in Archery and were economically dependent on him, he was "Mister Earl" — in a Southern combination of familiarity and deference, harkening back to the original master-slave relationship. (His wife is still called "Miss Lillian," and Jimmy is, of course, "Mister Jimmy.") Earl Carter was still the master and, recognizing him as such, the blacks in Archery kept their distance. In his autobiography Jimmy tells a story that serves as a good illustration of how this distance was maintained. On the night of the second Joe Louis — Max Schmeling prizefight the Carter's black neighbors came over to ask if they could listen to the fight on the Carter's battery operated radio. The fight had "heavy racial overtones" because Joe Louis had a chance to become the new black heavyweight champion of the world. Schmeling had beaten him in a previous fight, but in this fight Louis came out the winner, and Jimmy's father was "deeply disappointed." The black neighbors reacted in the following manner:

> There was no sound from anyone in the yard, except a polite, "Thank you, Mister Earl," offered to my father.
>
> Then, our several dozen visitors filed across the dirt road across the railroad track, and quietly entered a house about a hundred yards away out in the field. At that point, pandemonium broke loose inside that house, as our black neighbors shouted and yelled in celebration of the Louis victory. But all the curious, accepted proprieties of a racially- segregated society had been carefully observed.[6]

The black leader of the Archery community was the Bishop William Johnson of the African-Methodist-Episcopal Church. The bishop had a religious following among blacks in other states, and Jimmy recalls his funeral as the most exciting event that ever happened in Archery. "Preachers and choirs came from everywhere, and the whole settlement was amazed at the stream of big black Cadillacs, Packards, and Lincolns which had come from other states. Dozens of his white friends from the surrounding communities attended the services."[7] Yet even Bishop Johnson did not dare to come to the front door of the Carter house. Instead he would park in front of Jimmy's father's store and send one of his drivers to the back door to tell him that he wished to speak with him. The only black who violated this custom of segregationist society was Bishop Johnson's son. But then he was different. He had lived and been educated in the North, and so whenever he came to visit, he came to the front door. Jimmy's mother would receive him in the living room, while his father left and tried to pretend that it wasn't happening.

Jimmy's parents differed on the question of how blacks should be treated: he was a segregationist, while she had a liberal attitude, which was admittedly ahead of her time and would not come into its own until the civil rights movement of the 1960s. As a registered nurse, she took care of the black families, but more than this, she was perhaps the only one in Plains who demonstrated a general feeling of fellowship for blacks. "No one has ever been a stranger to me," she says now. In his autobiography, Jimmy sums up the difference between his parents thus: "He was quite conservative, and my mother was and is a liberal, but within our family we never thought about trying to define such labels."[8]

Growing up as he did in a predominantly black community, it was natural that most of Jimmy's friends were black. They worked in the fields together and played together — riding mules and horses through the fields, and fishing, swimming, and wrestling. But they didn't go to the same church or the same school, and they didn't sit together on the two-car diesel train that went to Americus, 13 miles away. He was "Mister Jimmy" just as his father was "Mister Earl." Later he would recall, "We would play together as children, then something would happen at about age twelve or 14. Suddenly when you're playing, he [black playmate] would step back and open a gate for you or you wouldn't do certain things together anymore. Then in later years, you'd go off to college or a job, and he would stay. And everyone kind of expected that."[9] It was only after he had left home that the mores of the segregationist society of his youth began to trouble him. He remembers only one racial argument with his father, which occurred when he was home on leave from submarine duty in 1950. After this, however, they both avoided the subject. Jimmy apparently thought too much of his father to challenge him on this issue.

Jimmy's rural boyhood had its Tom Sawyer aspects. He and his black playmates "rolled steel barrel hoops with a heavy wire pusher, slid down pine straw hills on old disc plow blades, hunted with sling shots and flips, flew homemade kites and Junebugs on a string, and threw spinning projectiles made of corn cobs and chicken feathers. We dug honey out of bee trees and harvested wild plums, blackberries, persimmons, chufas, and sassafras roots. We built dams on small streams, and tree houses where we lived overnight or for weekends. We hunted arrowheads in the fields."[10]

It was a life spent mostly in the woods and in the fields, an isolated life with little contact with the outside world. The Carters made trips to Columbus, Georgia, to visit Jimmy's mother's family, and Jimmy occasionally went with his mule-trader uncle to Atlanta to buy mules. But for the most part, Plains, with a population of a little over 500, was a metropolis for Jimmy.

There was not a great deal to do in Plains, and Jimmy only went there when he had to. His father's mother, Nina, lived in a large house by herself in town, and each night one of the various grandchildren would spend the night with her. Jimmy's grandmother seems to have been the only one in the family with the slightest hint of Southern eccentricity; he describes her as "very pretty, quite old-fashioned, vain about her age and appearance." In any case, his night was Friday, and on these Friday evenings he got to know some of the girls in town; his first date was with his grandmother's next-door neighbor. He was 13 at the time, and borrowed the family pickup truck for the occasion.

In Plains, Jimmy saw medicine shows, log-cutting contests, and circuses. The town had a small bowling alley, but no movie theater. When Jimmy and his cousin Hugh wanted to go to the movies, they had to hitchhike to Americus, 13 miles away. Since neither boy received an allowance, each had to earn his own spending money. From the time he was five years old, Jimmy sold bags of boiled peanuts on the streets of Plains. Later when he was in high school, he went into partnership with his cousin in the sale of hamburgers and homemade ice cream. As a peanut salesman Jimmy devised a method of distinguishing between the good and bad people of Plains — the good ones were, of course, the ones who bought peanuts from him. He also showed himself to be a shrewd businessman like his father. He usually made $1 a day selling peanuts Monday through Saturday and $5 on Sunday. By the time he was nine years old, he had saved enough money to buy several bales of cotton at a very low price. Selling them when the price went up again, he was able to purchase five houses, from which he collected a total of $16.50 monthly in rent until he left home for the Naval Academy.

It was a hard workingman's world, and Jimmy entered into it at a young age. However, the influence of two women helped relieve some of the grimness of his early life. One was his mother. Lillian Carter has a very loving nature, and has always shown great compassion for those who were sick or otherwise afflicted. Her recollections of Jimmy's boyhood are somewhat gentler than his own, perhaps because she does not like to think of his having had to endure any hardships. "The children had an easy life," she says now, "We wanted them to be happy. They went to the movies every Saturday." Undoubtedly, she did want the children to be happy; her tenderness provided a balance to Jimmy's father's strictness.

Today Jimmy feels that he is much more like his mother than his father. He obviously inherited some of the sterner aspects of his father's nature, but these were combined with his mother's deep sympathy for the weak and the poor. It was also from his mother that Jimmy got his love of reading. During the Depression years, Lillian Carter helped support the family by working 12 to 20 hours a day as a registered nurse at a nearby hospital or in patients' homes. She also served as a sort of community doctor for neighbors and the family. However, when she wasn't working or doing household chores, she read. "She read day and night. At the breakfast table — lunch table, supper table." And so did Jimmy, only he liked to lie on his stomach on an ottoman and read. His brother and sisters read too; the only one who didn't read was Jimmy's father, who couldn't, his mother says, because of poor eyesight. Whenever he was asked what he wanted for Christmas or his birthday, Jimmy would answer, "books." Aged four, he received a set of the complete works of Guy de Maupassant from his godmother. Then when he was 12, his teacher at school called him in and told him that he was ready to read *War and Peace*. Because of the title, he thought it was a book about cowboys and Indians, and he was therefore very disappointed when he checked the book out of the library, and he saw that it was over 1,000 pages long and not about cowboys and Indians at all. Nevertheless, he read it and says that it turned out to be one of his favorite books — one which he has reread several times since.

The teacher who gave Jimmy *War and Peace* to read was the other woman who touched his life at this time. She was Miss Julia Coleman, the superintendent at Plains High School. It was she who encouraged Jimmy and the rest of her students to learn about cultural things that weren't part of the normal rural school curriculum. Of her Jimmy has written,

> As a school boy who lived in an isolated farm community, my exposure to classical literature, art, and music was insured by this superlative teacher. She prescribed my reading list and gave me a silver star for

every five books and a gold star for ten book reports.

Miss Julia remains alive in my memory. She was short and somewhat crippled, yet she was quite graceful as she moved along. Her face was expressive, particularly when she was reading one of the poems she loved, or presenting to a class the paintings of Millet, Gainsborough, Whistler, or Sir Joshua Reynolds.[11]

Encouraged to read by his mother and Miss Julia Coleman, Jimmy learned of other ideas, of other worlds beyond the narrow one in which he grew up. "He was an ordinary country boy," his mother says now. Yet unlike so many other country boys who rebelled against their upbringing and fled to the city, Jimmy chose to remain in touch with the values of his childhood. "I had a stability there," he recalls, "You know, when things started going wrong in my own life, my mother and father were there, and my sisters and brothers were there, and the church was there, and my community was there — which never did change; never has changed yet — but there was something around which I built my life."[12]

Thomas Wolfe notwithstanding, Jimmy Carter believes that one can go home again; he always has.

CHAPTER 2

Jimmy and the Admiral

Jimmy Carter didn't always want to be president. If you had asked the sandy-haired five-year-old what he wanted to do when he grew up, he would have said, "I want to go to Annapolis." Later when he was at Annapolis, if you had asked him the same question again, he would have told you that he wanted to be chief of naval operations. He has always thought big, but in his early years this meant a military career.

The South has a long tradition of distinguished military service. Jimmy's father served in World War I as a first lieutenant in the army, but it was the navy that attracted Jimmy. His uncle, Tom Gordy, an enlisted man in the navy, sent the family postcards of exotic ports of call, and these cards no doubt set Jimmy dreaming of faraway places. He wasn't the first small-town boy to respond to the navy's lure of adventure. The navy was a way out of Plains, a way to see the world. It was also the way to a college education — something that no one in his family had ever had. Growing up during the Depression, Jimmy could not be sure that his family would be able to finance a college education, but if he went to Annapolis the government would help pay the bill.

13

Once he had decided to go to Annapolis, he immediately began to prepare himself so that when the time came, he would not be found lacking. While still in grammar school, Jimmy wrote to find out the admissions requirements, and practically memorized the Naval Academy catalogue when it arrived. He then planned a course of study in line with the requirements. As he recalls in his autobiography, "I had ridiculous and secret fears that I would not meet the requirements.

"Some of the physical requirements listed in the catalogue gave me deep concern. 'Malocclusion of teeth' was my biggest theoretical problem. When I ate fruit, the knowledge that my teeth did not perfectly meet interfered with my enjoying the flavor."[1] Later when he did get his appointment, Jimmy was upset by a doctor's report that he was underweight for the navy, and also had flat feet. To gain weight he stuffed himself with bananas, and to develop arches he rolled his feet over Coke bottles for many hours every week.

He reports these fears with humor, but it is obvious that at the time he took them very seriously. Even as a boy Jimmy was not one to undertake anything lightly. Having once established his goal, he set out to achieve it through careful planning and hard work — an approach he would demonstrate many times in his adult life.

Graduating from Plains High School at 16, Jimmy went to Georgia Southwestern College in nearby Americus for a year before going on to Georgia Tech as a Naval ROTC student. From there it was on to Annapolis, where he had won an appointment for the year 1943. At Annapolis his "lifetime commitment" carried him through both pangs of homesickness and the hazing to which all freshmen or "plebes" were subjected. Academically, he did well in spite of the intense competition. He had somewhat of a head start having spent one year at junior college and one year at Georgia Tech. He writes, "The academic requirements were stringent, but in my opinion not so difficult as at Georgia Tech."[2] In addition to the required engineering curriculum, he continued the liberal arts studies encouraged by his mother and Miss Julia Coleman, reading books in the areas of literature, philosophy, theology, art, and music. He and his roommate used part of their earnings as midshipmen to buy classical phonograph records, and, together with other midshipmen, they "would argue for hours about the relative quality of performance of orchestras and concert soloists." He was still very much the farm boy, hungry for knowledge and culture. Jimmy's mother remembers the beautiful letters he wrote her from Annapolis, adding that she must have suspected at the time that he would make something of himself, because she saved every one of them.

Jimmy's last years at Annapolis coincided with the end of World War II, and he remembers being at sea in the North Atlantic as part of a summer training cruise when he first heard the news that atomic bombs had been dropped on Hiroshima and Nagasaki. As he re-creates the moment: "Hundreds of sailors sat on the steel decks in front of the ship's loudspeakers, and we listened to the flat voice of President Truman as he gave us the incomprehensible description of the new atomic weapon which had just been dropped on Japan. There was no way to understand the meaning of the nuclear weapons used in the attack on the two Japanese cities. We had never heard even a rumor of this quantum leap in destructive power."[3]

In an interview with Bill Moyers, Jimmy also remembered feeling tremendous relief that the bombs had been chosen instead of a massive U.S. troop invasion of Japan. Asked if he would have been able to make the same decision Truman made, he replied, "Yes, I believe so. I would use every resource in my life to prevent it. But I think I would have that capacity to make a choice between the lesser of two evils, and, in my opinion, that was the kind of choice that Truman had to make."[4]

In 1946 Jimmy graduated from Annapolis in the top 10% of his class—no mean accomplishment for a boy from a rural Georgia background. The Naval Academy yearbook described him thus: "Studies never bothered Jimmy. In fact, the only times he opened his books were when his classmates desired help on problems. This lack of study did not, however, prevent him from standing in the upper part of his class. Jimmy's many friends will remember him for his cheerful disposition and his ability to see the humorous side of any situation."[5]

Summing up his three years at the Naval Academy, Jimmy writes, "I enjoyed it all, even the less pleasant parts. It was a time of challenge, excitement, and learning." *Challenge* is the key word in this description. Jimmy uses it frequently in recalling his service in the navy, and it is clear that it was this aspect that appealed to him the most. It also accounts for his tremendous admiration of Admiral Rickover, for the admiral presented him with a challenge that has haunted him ever since: Why not the best?

After graduation Jimmy briefly returned to Plains to marry Rosalynn Smith. He and Rosalynn had known each other all their lives. Their families were close, and

Rosalynn was best friends with Jimmy's younger sister, Ruth. But neither took much notice of the other until Jimmy, home from Annapolis for a visit, asked Rosalynn for a date. They went out to a movie with Ruth and her beau, and by the end of the evening Jimmy had decided that Rosalynn was the girl he wanted to marry. The next Christmas they saw each other constantly, and Jimmy proposed. Rosalynn turned him down at first, but later that year accepted, and they made July wedding plans. She was 17 at the time and enrolled as a freshman at Georgia Southwestern, where she was studying to become an interior decorator. Jimmy's proposal changed her plans. "I guess I always idolized him," she recalls, "He was older and so good looking. But I don't know what made me fall in love with him. I don't remember. I just loved him, that's all."[6]

With his new bride, Jimmy returned to accept his first assignment on an experimental radar and gunnery ship, operating out of Norfolk, Virginia. The sorry condition of the postwar navy discouraged him, and he says he would have resigned had he not, as an Annapolis graduate, been serving "at the pleasure of the president." In any event, he completed his two required years of surface duty and applied for submarine duty. From 1948 to 1953 when he left the navy, Jimmy served on submarines.

Submarine duty was "tough, dangerous, and demanding," and some men cracked under the strain. Jimmy tells of one of the electrician's mates who went mad with claustrophobia after they had been submerged for about three weeks. "We fed him intravenously and strapped him in a bunk to restrain him, which I am sure did not help his affliction. We finally had to surface, and transferred him to a helicopter a few hundred miles south of Bermuda. He never went back on a submarine."[7]

The danger involved in submarine duty appealed to Jimmy. Once he nearly lost his life when a giant wave swept him off the submarine bridge. The wave receded, and he found himself back on the deck of the submarine, thirty feet from where he had originally been standing. He also liked the comraderie brought about by long hours under water: "What I liked about being in the submarine is that it was embryonic. There was a feeling of personal privacy because of the closeness. People respected the privacy of others more. But there was also a sharing of responsibility. It was for me, a time of unreserved masculine behavior. There was on the submarine, once we pushed off for several months, a kind of liberation from the restraints of civilized life. There was a degeneration of behavior, a closeness just among men which I liked."[8]

Some of the men who served with Jimmy during these years remember him as "brainy," with a good grasp of technical matters, and a "gung ho" attitude about his job. They also describe him as a determined guy and a man of steel. As a junior officer aboard his first sub, the USS *Pomfret*, Jimmy refused to let seasickness get in the way of his work. Warren Colegrove, who was the *Pomfret*'s engineering officer, recalls, "He'd take his vomit bucket with him to the bridge. He was a gutsy guy." Retired Navy Captain John B. Williams has said that Jimmy was "one of the finest young junior officers we had," predicting that if he hadn't left the Navy he would be an admiral today.

The first submarines that Jimmy served on were conventional ones, powered by steam and required to surface periodically for refueling. However, the navy was just beginning to develop its first nuclear-powered subs. Because the steam that propelled these subs was produced by a controlled atomic pile, they would be able to travel around the world without refueling. The use of atomic power was thus a revolutionary development, equal in significance to the transition from manual to steam power, which had occurred near the end of the nineteenth century. The man chiefly responsible for this revolutionary development of atomic power was Admiral Hyman Rickover.

Rickover had worked on the development of the atomic bomb at the Atomic Energy Commission's Manhattan Project at Oak Ridge, Tennessee. After his Oak Ridge assignment, he and four other officers from Oak Ridge toured atomic research installations. They became convinced that it was possible to build a nuclear-powered submarine and submitted construction plans to the navy. The plans were set aside, but this didn't discourage Rickover. He continued to push until finally he persuaded the chief of naval operations, Admiral Chester Nimitz, to write a letter attesting to the military desirability of nuclear-powered submarines. He also got a statement from the Atomic Energy Commission as to the practicality of an atomic-powered engine. As a result of his constant prodding, Rickover won an appointment as head of the newly created atomic submarine division of the Bureau of Ships. He immediately began work on the first nuclear subs.

Jimmy applied to the nuclear submarine program as soon as he heard about it. He was interviewed by Admiral Rickover, and the story of that interview is one he never seems to tire of telling. The question asked at the end of the interview became the title of his autobiography and also of the speech in which he announced his presidential candidacy. Here is the story as Jimmy tells it:

It was the first time I met Admiral Rickover, and we sat in a large room by ourselves for more than two hours, and he let me choose any subject I wished to discuss. Very carefully, I chose those about which I knew most at the time — current events, seamanship, music, literature, naval tactics, electronics, gunnery — and he began to ask me a series of questions of increasing difficulty. In each instance, he soon proved that I knew relatively little about the subject I had chosen.

He always looked right into my eyes, and he never smiled. I was saturated with cold sweat.

Finally, he asked me a question and I thought I could redeem myself. He said, "How did you stand in your class at the Naval Academy?" Since I had completed my sophomore year at Georgia Tech before entering Annapolis as a plebe, I had done very well, and I swelled my chest with pride and answered, "Sir, I stood fifty-ninth in a class of 820!" I sat back to wait for the congratulations — which never came. Instead, the question: "Did you do your best?" I started to say "Yes, sir," but I remembered who this was, and recalled several of the many times at the Academy when I could have learned more about our allies, our enemies, weapons, strategy, and so forth. I was just human. I finally gulped and said, "No, sir, I didn't *always* do my best."

He looked at me for a long time, and then turned his

chair around to end the interview. He asked one final
question, which I have never been able to forget—or to
answer. He said, "Why not?" I sat there for a while,
shaken, and then slowly left the room.[9]

Accepted to the program, Jimmy was ordered to
Schenectady as senior officer of the pre-commissioning
crew of *Seawolf*, one of the first atomic submarines to be
built. During the day he taught mathematics and reactor
technology to the crew members; at night for one semes-
ter he took graduate courses in reactor technology and
nuclear physics at Union College in Schenectady. In the
1976 presidential campaign he would describe himself as a
nuclear physicist on the basis of these courses. Since he
never received a degree, *nuclear engineer* was the appropriate term. Still, as political writer David Nordan
pointed out, "But let's face it. In Plains, Ga., a fellow who
did graduate work in physics and ran a nuclear submarine
is a nuclear physicist— whether a Ph.D. from MIT agrees
with that or not."[10]

More important, perhaps, than any courses Jimmy took
at this time was the contact with Rickover. In his autobiography he writes, "He may not have cared or known
it, certainly not at that time, but Admiral Rickover had a
profound effect on my life — perhaps more than anyone
except my own parents."[11] It was not that there was any
close personal relationship between the two men, but
rather, "It was an impersonal demand of a
perfectionist . . . he demanded from me a standard of
performance, and a depth of commitment, that I had
never realized before that I could achieve."[12]

Rickover once summed up his philosophy thus: "The more you sweat in peace, the less you bleed in war." Possessed of an almost superhuman energy, he drove himself and his men mercilessly. Of him Jimmy writes:

> He was unbelievably hardworking and competent, and he demanded total dedication from his subordinates. We feared and respected him and strove to please him. I do not in that period remember his ever saying a complimentary word to me. The absence of a comment was his compliment; he never hesitated to criticize severely if a job were not done as well as he believed it could be done. He expected the maximum from us, but he always contributed more.
>
> Once, I remember flying to Seattle with him at the end of a hard day's work. It was a long flight in the commercial propjet plane. He began to work when the plane took off, and we were determined to do the same. After a few hours the rest of us gave up and went to sleep. When we awoke, Rickover was still working.[13]

Those who worked with Jimmy when he was governor and later during his 1976 presidential campaign verified that he followed the example set by Admiral Rickover. Hamilton Jordan, his campaign manager in '76, said, "He [Carter] expects us to be like him — well-disciplined, well-organized perfectionists." Another staffer confided that he and the others were beginning to hate Rickover because, while Jimmy thought he was Rickover, none of them thought they were Jimmy Carter. Still another said, "I've really learned what it takes to be successful — work your ass off." *Newsweek* called Jimmy "the first bionic candidate — a clockwork politician who gets up earlier, turns in later, burns more jet fuel, exhausts more shoe leather, squeezes more hands, eyeballs more eyeballs, grins more grins and believes more serenely in himself than anyone in the Democratic class of '76."[14]

Jimmy also clearly admired the boldness with which Rickover pursued his goals. He writes that Rickover "was never tactful or timid in his demands upon the Congress, the navy, or the manufacturers who supplied the thousands of equipment parts of unprecedented design." Similarly, Jimmy was neither tactful nor timid in his dealings with the state legislature when he was governor. Admiral Rickover practically turned the navy upside down to get the nuclear submarine program going, and the same could be said of Jimmy with his government reorganization program. Both men "battled tirelessly, never without criticism" to achieve their goals.

Still, Rickover's influence on Jimmy should not be overemphasized. The actual period they worked together was relatively short — somewhat less than a year. During this time Rickover had an impact on Jimmy because he was a more sophisticated version of Jimmy's father, also a stern and hardworking man. Meeting Rickover didn't change Jimmy's life; rather it reinforced what he had already learned from his childhood — that those who work hard are those who come out on top.

On the whole, Jimmy's years in the navy left their mark on his character. They increased his self-discipline, and they may also have contributed to the uncompromising streak in his character. As Jack Spalding, editor of the

Atlanta Journal has written of Jimmy: "He's a little stiff-necked in public, untaught in the art of compromise, a spot of the Naval Academy still is visible and the quarterdeck touch is with him yet."[15] Tom Murphy, Speaker of the Georgia House during part of Jimmy's term as governor, has gone even further. He has said that Jimmy "tried to run the state the same way he once commanded a Navy submarine—his way or else [in actual fact, Jimmy was never a submarine commander because he never acquired enough seniority to have a ship of his own]. He never asked for any advice, any suggestions, he just gave orders."[16] Again, as with Rickover, the experience in the navy served to strengthen the qualities of self-discipline and respect for authority, which Jimmy had developed as a farm boy, growing up under the watchful eyes of a strict father.

After ten years in the navy, Jimmy was indeed in a good position. As he writes in his autobiography, "My job was the best and most promising in the navy, and the work was challenging and worthwhile. The salary was good, and the retirement benefits were liberal and assured. The contact with Admiral Rickover alone made it worthwhile." He had every reason to remain in the navy, and yet he left. The specific event which led him to resign and return to civilian life was his father's death from cancer in 1953. Returning to Plains to be with his father before he died, Jimmy saw the significance in his father's life: "Hundreds of people came by to speak to Daddy, or to bring him a choice morsel of food or some fresh flowers. It was obvious that he meant much to them, and it caused me to compare my prospective life with his. . . .

"I began to think about the relative significance of his life and mine. He was an integral part of the community, and had a wide range of varied but interrelated interests and responsibilities. He was his own boss, and his life was stabilized by the slow and evolutionary changes in the local societal structure."[17]

The choice that confronted Jimmy was this: "Did I want to be the Chief of Naval Operations, and devote my whole life to that one narrowly defined career, which was a good one—or did I want to go back and build a more diverse life with a lot of friends, permanent stability in a community, an interrelationship in the life of a whole group of people . . ."[18] He chose the latter, but only after a heated argument with his wife. For Rosalynn, Plains represented narrowness rather than life in the navy. And in some ways perhaps she was right. Yet it was the very narrowness of Plains that Jimmy needed. The navy had given him an opportunity to see the world, but now he was ready — in his words — to resubmit his ties to his birthplace. He probably would have gone back to Plains eventually even if his father hadn't died. Plains represented the secure and stable environment of his boyhood, and he would always return to it to gather strength for his next foray into the world.

Much later he would look back on the years in the navy, years that were also the last years of his father's life, and say:

"Well, I would like, obviously, in retrospect, to have been more with my father. I never thought he would die so young. But I've never regretted a day that I served in the Navy. That was an opportunity for me that paid off. . . .

I stretched my mind, and had a great challenge, and I never had any regret for a single day that I spent in the Navy. I never regretted getting out a single day after I left."[19]

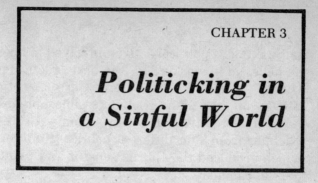

CHAPTER 3

Politicking in a Sinful World

When Jimmy Carter was thinking of running for state senator, he had a talk with a visiting minister, in town for the church's annual revival services. The minister believed that politics was far from an honorable profession, and he urged Jimmy not to become involved in it. He suggested that if Jimmy really wanted to be of service to people, he should join the ministry or do social work. Carter replied, "How would you like to be pastor of a church with 80,000 members?"[1] The minister finally agreed that one could be a politician and still remain a Christian. In Carter's own mind the two callings clearly were not incompatible. Later, as governor of Georgia, he would say in an address to the Youth for Christ of Metropolitan Atlanta: "I'm a politician and a Christian and I see no conflict." Then he quoted Reinhold Niebuhr, his favorite theologian, who defined politics as the sad art of establishing justice in a sinful world.

Carter's reference to Niebuhr is significant because in his own career Niebuhr successfully combined religious and political activity. As a Protestant theologian, he stressed man's fallen state and the need for hard-won faith; but as a political activist involved in liberal causes, he believed in working for the best practical possibility. Other public officials before Carter, notably Adlai Stevenson, had found Niebuhr's philosophy of Christian realism attractive. However, Jimmy Carter came to Niebuhr from a far different political tradition than that which produced the Illinois senator and two-time presidential candidate.

That tradition is Southern populism. In the late 1800s farmers and factory workers became increasingly discontented, as they became aware of the tremendous gulf that existed between their incomes and those of the Eastern financial and industrial titans. The Populist movement pitted the farmers of the West and the South against these Eastern magnates, and made an appeal to workers everywhere. As the New South, which emerged after the Civil War, began to lean closer and closer toward the industrial North, South Georgia became a hotbed of agrarian discontent. Making political capital out of this mood of dissatisfaction were two Populist demagogues. The first was Tom Watson (1856-1922). He became the champion of poor white farmers. He was elected to Congress and later, having lost his seat in the House, won a place in the Senate. A fiery orator who lashed out against trusts and capitalist finance, Watson was also known later on for his violent anti-Negro rhetoric. He was followed by Eugene Talmadge (1884-1946). Talmadge established himself as the dirt farmer's candidate and proponent of white supremacy; he was elected governor four times. Rural voters knew that Talmadge was their man when they saw him drive up to a courthouse in his horse and buggy, dislodge a fly from the horse's ear with a well-

aimed squirt of tobacco juice, and snap his crimson gal-
luses (suspenders) before getting out.

These then were two important political leaders who
came out of South Georgia. Tom Watson died two years
before Carter was born, but as a boy he must have heard a
great deal about him because his grandfather, Jack
Gordy, was an ardent supporter of the Sage of Hickory
Hill. Talmadge's career was in full swing when Jimmy
was a teenager, so he had a chance to observe the Wild
Man of Sugar Creek firsthand. Jimmy's grandfather had a
keen interest in politics. Although he never ran for public
office, he did serve as postmaster under four different
presidential administrations — a feat which required a
certain amount of political maneuvering. His grandfather
also came up with the idea of Rural Free Mail Delivery,
and prodded Watson as his congressman to get federal
legislation passed, making RFD a reality.

Jimmy's father also became involved in politics, especially toward the end of his life. He was elected to the
state legislature, where he served in the House one year
before his death. He encouraged his son to attend local
political rallies, and Jimmy recalls one in which a candidate for the U.S. Senate was upstaged by a bread-slicing
machine — the first that people in that part of the state
had ever seen. As a boy he listened to political conven-
tions on the family's battery operated radio, and he remembers that when the battery went dead during the
1936 Republican Convention, they took the radio outside
and hooked it up to the car battery in order to hear
Landon's nomination.

Later when Jimmy was in Washington on naval duty,
he would look up two senators from his home state, Wal-

ter F. George and Richard B. Russell. However, aside
from these brief contacts the political seed sown in his
boyhood lay dormant. It would not bear fruit until he
returned to Plains after his father's death in 1953.

Jimmy's first years back home were not easy. In 1954,
there was a drought, which meant failure of the peanut
crop. In that year the business netted only $184. Realizing
that he actually knew little about farming, Jimmy read
books on the subject, talked to local experts, and took
short courses at the Agricultural Experiment station
nearby. Although she had three young children to raise,
Rosalynn helped with the business too. She kept the
books, weighed the fertilizer trucks, and did whatever
else she could. Gradually Jimmy built up the business,
continuing his father's practice of buying local farmers'
peanuts and then selling them in bulk to large processors.
By the early 1970s, the Carter Warehouse was grossing
$800,000 a year and the family owned, through various
partnerships, 2,500 acres in Sumter and Webster counties.

However, peanuts weren't the only problem in those
years. The South to which the Carters returned was in
the initial throes of the civil rights movement, launched
by the Supreme Court decision outlawing segregation in
the schools. In the wake of that decision, White Citizens'
Councils were formed to fight for the continuance of segregation. Thus one day Jimmy was visited at his peanut
warehouse by the local chief of police and the Baptist
minister, who asked if he would join the citizens' council
they were organizing. He refused, and did so again when
they returned a few days later to inform him that he was
the only white citizen who hadn't joined. They came back

again — this time with several friends of his who were also customers — and warned that it would be bad for his business if he didn't join. They even offered to lend him the necessary $5 dues. Carter turned them down, and his business was indeed boycotted, but fortunately only for a short time.

When the civil rights movement was in full swing in the 1960s, some activist groups tried to integrate the churches. The Plains Baptist Church, which Jimmy and his family attended, voted as to whether or not they should continue to exclude blacks. The Carter family — Jimmy, his wife, their two sons, and his mother — plus one other family were the only ones who voted in favor of allowing blacks to worship in the church. The Carters' vote and Jimmy's outspoken opinion in favor of admitting blacks caused fellow worshippers to give the family the cold shoulder for a while.

There was trouble again in 1964 when Lillian Carter was running the local Johnson-for-President office. At this time her car was vandalized, and Jimmy's son Chip was beaten up for wearing an L.B.J. button at school.

In this racially charged atmosphere, Carter made his political debut. Like his father he started out by joining various public service groups. He became state president of the Certified Seed Organization, district governor of the Lions International, chairman of the local Planning Commission, and later president of the Georgia Planning Association. He also served on the county library board and the hospital authority.

More important, however, from a political standpoint, was Jimmy's appointment to the Sumter County School Board. As a member of the board and later its chairman,

Carter came under attack for his liberal attitudes. However, as *Wall Street Journal* Atlanta Bureau chief Neil Maxwell points out, by today's standards Carter does not seem too different from the staunch segregationists on the board.[2] For example, when a group of white citizens came to protest the planned location of a black school as being too close to a white school, Carter proposed a measure relocating the black school. He did not object to the fact that white teachers got sick pay while their black counterparts did not, and he voted for a proposal to use the surplus funds from the sick leave account to give white teachers a raise, but not black teachers. At no time during the six years he served on the board did he do anything to help enforce the Supreme Court decision outlawing segregation. Then as now it was difficult to categorize Jimmy. Says W.W. Foy, who was school superintendent at the time, "I would say he was more of a conservative than a liberal in most respects, but he was a lot more liberal than his neighbors."[3] There is no doubt that, like the rest of the members of the board, Carter was a segregationist. However, unlike some who didn't want to do anything for black schools, he demonstrated a genuine concern for improving the quality of education for blacks. He was involved in the planning of new black schools, and he also pushed for a plan to consolidate the county and city of Americus school systems, which he felt would help raise the overall academic caliber.

Since the school merger plan had to be approved by the people, Carter made speeches in favor of it throughout the county, thus getting his first taste of campaigning. His opponents were led by his cousin Hugh Carter (now a state senator). They accused Jimmy Carter of being an integrationist. Although the plan did call for separate schools for blacks and whites, his opponents believed that there would be more pressure to integrate one system rather than two. In the end the plan was voted down, and Carter suffered his first political defeat, which he describes as a "stinging disappointment." Yet characteristically, defeat only caused him to work harder. In this instance, it also caused him to set his sights on a seat in the state legislature, where he felt he could accomplish more.

In 1953 when Jimmy's father died, his seat in the legislature had been offered to Jimmy's mother, who had turned it down. A decade later she would be elected as a delegate to the Democratic convention pledged to Lyndon Johnson and would help her son in his campaigns. But she apparently had no wish to become involved in politics at that time. The fact that she was offered her husband's seat, however, does give an indication of her standing in the community. The seat went to one of Jimmy's father's close friends; and while Carter says he would not have challenged the friend for the seat, he admits that the thought did cross his mind several times in the years that followed.

In any event, Carter decided to run for the legislature in his own right in 1962, and it was this campaign that gave him his first view of political corruption. Entering the race at the last moment, he faced an opponent who had the backing of one of the county courthouse cliques, which were still a strong force in local politics. However, through vigorous campaigning, aided by family and friends, he was able to secure enough of a following to present a serious challenge to his opponent. On election day Carter made a point of visiting the various polling places, and what he saw going on at the one in Quitman County angered him a great deal. Here the local state legislator who supported his opponent all but marked the voter's ballots for them. When the tally was announced, it was clear that the votes cast in this county were the deciding factor in Carter's defeat. He and a young lawyer investigated the situation and discovered that among those who had voted for his opponent in Quitman County were residents of the local cemetery, people who were currently serving prison sentences, and others who had long since moved out of the county.

When the State Democratic Convention in Macon ignored Carter's challenge of the election results, he enlisted the help of John Pennington, an investigative reporter for the *Atlanta Journal*, who gave the case statewide publicity. Eventually it was brought to court and the judge declared that given the fraud in Quitman County, the votes cast there would not be considered. Thus on the basis of the tally in the other precincts, Carter was declared the winner. But a new law permitted appeal back to the local Democratic Executive Committee, and as this committee was controlled by the boss who had fixed the election in Quitman County, it was no great surprise when the committee decided in favor of Carter's opponent. Carter's lawyer, in turn, tracked down the state party chairman, J.B. Fuqua, who was hunting pheasant near the Canadian border. He presented Carter's case to Fuqua. With the general election only a few days away, Fuqua agreed that Carter's name should appear on the ballot as the Democratic nominee.

In the general election, Carter defeated his Republican opponent and took his seat in the senate. His most important victory had been over the local political bosses of his own party. In later campaigns he would denounce the powerful few who ran the party at the expense of the rank and file of voters. He had refused to let himself be intimidated by the bosses, and the stubborn determination he showed in his battle with them was a characteristic that would often be remarked on in his political career.

Carter had arrived at the state legislature by much the same path as his father, but here the similarity between them ended. For Jimmy had been out of state for over a decade, and these years away had given him a different perspective. They had tended to reinforce the liberal and humanitarian values he had learned from his mother. Thus he was destined to be more than just another country politician, seeking to take care of his own. In one of his maiden speeches in the senate, he urged the abolition of the infamous "thirty questions." These questions, which were so difficult that no one could answer them, were used in some counties to keep black voters away from the polls. His speech clearly represented a departure from the politics of his father, as well as from the racist gestures of past South Georgia politicians like Talmadge and Watson.

As a state senator, Carter showed the same attention to detail that he would later display as governor. He took his job seriously, and pledged to himself to read every bill before he voted on it. This was not an easy task since approximately 2,500 bills and resolutions were introduced each legislative session. To keep his promise, he took a speed-reading course, and in the process became an "expert on many unimportant subjects."

Education continued to be a major area of concern to

Carter. He hoped that eventually the quality of education throughout the state would become more equalized. To further this end, he proposed a plan to provide hardship aid to rural school systems like that of Sumter County, from which he had come. He served on the educational matters committee, on the higher education subcommittee, and was one of two legislators to serve on a blue ribbon commission created to study the needs and status of Georgia's educational system. The other member of the commission was Dr. Horace Tate, then executive director of the black state teachers' organization. Dr. Tate went on to become associate director of the integrated Georgia teachers' association, a state senator, and a supporter of Jimmy's when he ran for governor. The recommendations of this commission became Senate Bill 180 or the Minimum Foundation Program for Education, which upgraded the total educational program with increases in state spending. This legislation represented an updating of the Minimum Foundation Program passed in 1949 in an attempt to provide a minimum level of education through greater state expenditures. The passage of this bill in 1964 was considered a major achievement of Governor Carl Sanders' administration.

Carter also served on the agriculture and appropriations committees. On the latter he displayed a fiscally cautious outlook, typical of a legislator from a rural county. He was critical of the committee for looking only at proposals to finance new programs and failing to reexamine those that were already in existence. He also felt that too little time was spent studying budget items involving especially large amounts of money. Specifically, he opposed the construction of a new $6 million state office building, favored state rather than private ownership of the dorms on the state university campuses, and questioned the need for an expensive program of driver education.

Carter frequently clashed with lobbyists for special interest groups. He developed a healthy dislike for many of them because he felt that they did not represent the best interests of the average citizen. He opposed "sweetheart" bills which favored a particular individual in terms of salary or retirement benefits and he was against "special deal" pay hikes for state department heads who played politics. Instead he believed that uniform salaries for state officials should be established by a state salary commission. He pushed for legislation creating such a commission and lost, but later succeeded when he was governor.

During the two terms he served in the legislature, Carter earned a reputation as a moderate. He was well liked by his colleagues, who considered him to be one of the most outstanding members of the senate. Having made good in the state legislature, Carter began to think of running for Congress. His interest in securing a congressional seat had to do with certain political dislocations that were going on in the state at the time. Traditionally Georgia had been a solidly Democratic state, but there was such disenchantment with the civil rights programs of President Lyndon Johnson that Republican Barry Goldwater carried the state in 1964. In the same year Howard "Bo" Callaway, also a Republican, was elected to Congress from Jimmy's own district in Southwest Georgia. Callaway was the first Republican to be elected to Congress from Georgia in 100 years. Thus in the spring of

1966, Carter decided to launch a campaign to unseat the popular Callaway. In his autobiography he acknowledges that he was motivated to a certain extent by "natural competitiveness" with Callaway: "He [Callaway] had graduated from West Point just about the same time I completed my work at Annapolis. When I was a state senator, one of my major projects was to secure a four-year college in Southwest Georgia. As a member of the University System Board of Regents, Callaway tried unsuccessfully to block the college. He was leader of the Young Republicans, and in some ways I had become the leader among the Georgia's Young Democrats. When we were around each other, both of us were somewhat tense."[4]

As things turned out, however, Callaway decided to quit his congressional seat and run for governor. It looked to be a close race between Callaway and former Governor Ernest Vandiver. However, Vandiver had suffered a heart attack during his 1959-1963 term as governor and was advised by his doctor that it would be hazardous to his health to run. He withdrew from the race. At this point Carter decided to pass up a sure-thing seat in Congress and try for the governorship. He entered a crowded field, and he entered it late. Besides himself there were five contenders for the nomination in the Democratic camp: former Lieutenant Governor Garland Byrd; James Gray, a newspaper publisher and TV station owner who was an avowed segregationist; Lester Maddox, an Atlanta restaurant owner who had closed down his place rather than serve blacks; Hoke O'Kelly, a perennial candidate who seemed to run just for the hell of it; and Ellis Arnall, a former governor (1943-1947). Of the six, Arnall was considered the favorite. His administration had been characterized by integrity and forward-looking policies, and he had the backing of the party moderates and the Atlanta press.

Unlike Arnall and the other candidates, Carter was relatively unknown. Yet as a "new face" he possessed a certain advantage. He was young (41 that year) and physically the most attractive of the candidates. People noticed his trim and fit appearance and remarked on his resemblance to John F. Kennedy. There was the same shock of hair, the boyish grin, and the same seriousness and quiet humor. Carter even shared Kennedy's habit of emphasizing points with jabs of an open hand.

He was supported by the Young Democrats, several fellow state senators, and a combination of others to whom he appeared a good and capable man. He was particulary popular with the young and with women. They loved him on college campuses when he spoke out against tuition increases; he pledged that if elected he would uphold academic freedom and called on them to become involved in government and correct its evils. Carter's strong legislative record in education also made him the choice of educators — 8 out of 10 members of the State Board of Education endorsed his candidacy.

During his first gubernatorial race, Carter sounded many of the notes that would become leitmotifs of his later campaigns. He said that it was time for the people rather than the political bosses to run the government, and he called for reorganization and fiscal prudence. He made honesty and openness issues, proclaiming that gubernatorial candidates should be "direct, truthful and talk common sense." At one point he said, "During this campaign you may well ask 'Jimmy Who?' and about my last name, but you will never have to ask 'Jimmy What?' about my last book or my last radio or TV appearance."[5] Addressing a group of teenagers, he brought up the question of trust: "If I ever let you down in my actions, I want you to let me know about it and I'll correct it. I promise never to betray your trust in me."

Carter also showed himself to be an indefatigable campaigner. He and his wife and his mother stumped the state, and in the course of the campaign Carter lost 22 pounds. Watching him campaign at this time, Charles Kirbo, an Atlanta lawyer who first helped Jimmy when he contested the '62 election and later became one of his top political advisors, sensed the winner in him. He observed how Carter listened to people and seemed to find some good in everyone. And indeed, in those few short months before the primary, Carter worked hard to shed the cloudy "Jimmy Who?" image and emerge as a known and liked political personality. He resisted being labeled liberal, conservative, or middle of the road, saying, "I believe that I'm a more complicated person than that." But the truth was that he and Ellis Arnall appealed to basically the same type of voter, "to those who would rather hear what the state can do than what the federal government has done, who would rather move forward than backward, who are optimists and believers in excellence."[6] Unfortunately for Carter, Arnall's territory was pretty much staked out for him, and thus it was up to Carter to capture it. Carter criticized the state constitution drawn up under Arnall's administration, arguing that it was so bad that it had to be amended over 200 times; called Arnall's plans for financing new programs "ridiculous"; and challenged both Arnall and another Democratic candidate, James Gray, to a debate on the issues. Nevertheless, he failed to differentiate himself sufficiently from Arnall to attract enough of the moderate vote. It was a mistake he would not make again.

Carter also suffered a disadvantage in terms of style. As Bruce Galphin noted in a story in the *Atlanta Constitution*, "the former governor [Arnall] knows how to weigh every word, every gesture; he can fight and laugh at the same time; he clearly enjoys the game. Beside Mr. Arnall's color, Mr. Carter's style is pale. His humor goes little beyond a bashful smile."[7]

In between endorsing Arnall and lambasting Lester Maddox, the Atlanta press managed to find time to take a look at Carter. Jack Spalding, editor of the *Atlanta Journal*, remembers that he liked Carter at the time, although officially the paper gave its endorsement to Arnall. Bruce Galphin also responded to Carter's appeal, even as he observed his political greenness." His description of Carter's appearance at the Atlanta Press Club offers a revealing portrait of the would-be governor at an important juncture of his career. Galphin wrote:

> It is hard to meet Sen. Jimmy Carter and hear him talk about state government without liking him and admiring his integrity. . . .For those who hadn't known Sen. Carter before, his appearance at the Atlanta Press Club Thursday was a startling experience. Here was a breed of politician new to Georgia's big contest: subdued, frank even about his deficiencies, refusing to torture the traditional whipping boys.
> When he got to talking about Milledgeville State

Hospital, he said the plight of patients there made him choke up, and indeed his voice faltered and his face reddened a shade. . . . He quoted Edmund Burke to the effect that services should be centralized but power decentralized. He spoke of a quest for excellence in state government, and he said he wanted to involve more of the public in the affairs of government.

But some of the assets of Jimmy Carter the man may be deficits for Jimmy Carter the political candidate.

His honesty is almost painful. He admitted the unique problems of big cities were new to him. He said he had been boning up on them in the past few weeks, and you could believe he can learn fast. But it was a deficiency, politically speaking, he shouldn't have admitted.

He said Viet Nam wasn't an issue in the Georgia governor's race — an honest position — but then went on to talk about it, to admit it was complex and finally to confess, "I don't have any solution." He would have done better to stop after saying it wasn't an issue.

It apparently didn't occur to Sen. Carter — as it had to Lester Maddox, Bo Callaway and Ellis Arnall before him — to pack the Press Club luncheon with friends. So the room was embarrassingly bare before TV camera eyes.[8]

Interestingly enough, one thing that stands out in this description is Carter's refusal to give simple answers — a trait he has retained even after becoming wiser in the ways of politics; and which, in the 1976 presidential campaign, led to accusations that he was vague on the issues. As Charles Kirbo remarked, "I've seen him keep talking until people misunderstand him. But I don't think he does it deliberately."

Despite these handicaps and the fact that he had little money or political organization, Carter made a good showing in the Democratic primary, coming in third with only 6,000 votes less than Lester Maddox, who finished second to Arnall. There were those who believed that if Carter had had at least three more weeks in which to campaign, he would have won. Many believed that if he had made it to the run-off, he would have been elected governor. As it was, Maddox beat Arnall in the run-off because many Republicans crossed over to vote for him, believing that Maddox would be the easier man for Callaway to beat in November. Unhappy with Maddox's victory, liberal-moderate Democrats organized a write-in campaign to provide an alternative to both Maddox and Callaway in the general election. There was some talk of Carter's being the write-in candidate, but in the end the group chose Arnall. Because of the write-in votes neither Maddox nor Callaway received a clear majority, though Callaway did come in ahead of Maddox. This meant that the state legislature (by an old law since changed) had the authority to choose the winner from the two front runners. The heavily Democratic legislature naturally chose Maddox.

Carter had little respect for Maddox, and thus it was a blow to him when the segregationist restaurant-owner became governor. If there was one thing he had learned about politicking in a sinful world, it was that he wasn't going to get much done in the way of establishing justice unless he got elected. And so the next time around he was determined to win. As he writes in his autobiography, "I waited about one month and then began campaigning again for governor. I remembered the admonition, 'You show me a good loser and I will show you a loser.' I did not intend to lose again."[9]

In 1966 Carter appeared to represent a new breed of Georgia politician. He came off as an idealistic young fellow who didn't resort to the usual tricks. Unfortunately, nice guys don't always finish first in the Cracker State. So four years later when he ran again, Carter would use some of the old-style tactics of his South Georgia forebears. In 1966 Carter was still politically naive; the 1970 campaign, however, marked his coming of age.

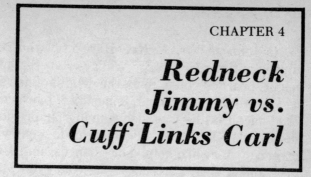

CHAPTER 4

Redneck Jimmy vs. Cuff Links Carl

Jimmy Carter's 1970 gubernatorial campaign is one of the most controversial aspects of his career. Many of the charges that he is a liar, hypocrite, and closet racist stem from this campaign. Thus it is worth examining in detail. What kind of a campaign did Carter run and why? These are important questions that need to be answered.

Most of Carter's best friends — with the exception of a few previous supporters and his family — advised him not to run for governor in 1970. They thought he should try for lieutenant governor or perhaps commissioner of agriculture. But having once made up his mind, nothing could deter Carter. As he writes in his autobiography, "There was never the slightest hesitancy on my part about what to do. I thought I could run and win, and I never worried at all about who else might be in the race against me."[1]

Who were his opponents? In a book called *The Southern Strategy*, Hal Gulliver and Reg Murphy describe the 1970 governor's race as "a topsy-turvy grab bag of candidates, an almost something-for-everyone kind of division.

"Among the candidates were a woman Socialist, Mrs.

Linda Jenness; Dr. McKee Hargrett, who referred to himself at times as 'George Wallace Hargrett'; Jan Cox, a bright, bearded young man, the delight of newsmen, who said he was running on an 'inner man' platform and confided once that he was also running for president of his motorcycle club, and he thought his entry into the governor's race had helped his chances; and, J.B. Stoner, a Savannah Beach attorney, the cold-eyed candidate of hate, who openly based his campaign on his dislike of Negroes and Jews."[2]

However, besides Jimmy Carter there were only two really serious Democratic contenders. One was C.B. King, a lawyer, who was the first black to try for the governorship since Reconstruction. The other was Carl Sanders, a lawyer and former governor (1962-1966). He was the "Ellis Arnall" of the 1970 campaign — the candidate who had money, a strong political backing, and a good record as a progressive. Sanders was clearly the man Carter had to beat

Two and a half years before the election, Carter was already taking a good look at his chief rival. Bill Shipp, associate editor of the *Atlanta Constitution*, cites a memo that Carter scribbled to an aide at this time. It went like this:

> Some images to be projected regarding Carl Sanders . . . More liberal, has close connections with Ivan Allen [then mayor of Atlanta] and Atlanta establishment . . . refuses to let Georgia Democrats have a voice in the Democratic party . . . Atlanta-oriented to the exclusion of other metro and rural areas . . . pretty boy . . . ignored prison reform opportunities . . . nouveau riche . . . refused to assist local school boards in school

financing . . . excluded George Wallace from state . . .

. . . You can see some of these are conflicting but right now we just need to collect all these rough ideas we can. Later we can start driving a wedge between me and him . . .[3]

But the real clincher in determining Carter's strategy against Sanders was a poll that Carter had done in 1969. William Hamilton, a top-flight Washington pollster, was hired to make a survey of Georgia voters. Hamilton's poll revealed some interesting things. One was that Carter did indeed face a formidable opponent in Carl Sanders, as one out of five voters rated him an excellent governor. The poll also showed that Carter himself had a recognition problem. In spite of the good showing he had made in 1966 and the campaigning he had done since then, he was still "Jimmy Who?" to many voters. Twenty-five percent of the electorate hadn't heard of him, and only 11 out of 20 Democrats had any opinion of him.

So far the picture didn't look very bright for Carter. But there was something else that showed up in the poll: both Sanders and Carter were viewed as a little more liberal than the majority of the electorate, but this was more true for Sanders than Carter. And further: "Of those voters who are aware of both men, it is that group of populistic staunch segregationists who see both Carter and Sanders as being too liberal. This suggests that neither candidate has made strong inroads into this group which is 12 to 15 per cent of the electorate. Sanders has the bigger problem because his past actions were better known to this group."[4]

Taking his cue from Hamilton's poll, Carter set out to

win the segregationist vote by trying to appeal to all those who supported Lester Maddox and George Wallace. (In the 1968 presidential election, Wallace had carried five Southern states and received 50% of the vote in Georgia.) His recognition problem actually began to work to his advantage. As a relative unknown without much of a past record, he was able to postion himself to the right of Sanders — though in fact he was the more liberal of the two. While Carter stressed the fact that he was a "redneck" and a conservative, Sanders was branded an ultraliberal and good friend of Hubert Humphrey. Sanders had in fact supported Humphrey in 1968, and Carter people were able to cause him some embarrassment when they discovered that Sanders' campaign buttons were actually recycled Humphrey buttons.

Carter also presented himself as the antiestablishment candidate. Hamilton's poll had shown that 27 percent of the undecided voters felt "Carl Sanders has become too close to the Atlanta bigwigs. . . . About one-fifth of the undecided believed that Sanders had become too citified, nationally, and Atlanta oriented. Carter said that the most important thing was "to regain control of our own affairs and the confidence of people in their own government and bring them to full life." He attacked Sanders as a pawn of the establishment and portrayed himself as the spokesman of all the "little people" in the state, whose voice was being ignored. His campaign slogan was "Isn't it time somebody spoke up for you?" And to go with this slogan on billboards and brochures, the Carter people selected the ugliest photograph of Carter they could find. It was calculated to show him as a grim-faced worker and the standard-bearer of the average voter, who, according to the poll was not young, not black, and not poor. It was the "real dirt farmer" pitch that had served Old Gene (Talmadge) so well before. Carter never went so far as to adopt the Cracker speech, which Talmadge used when campaigning in rural counties, but a television commercial did show him harvesting peanuts on his farm as the voice-over asked, "Can you imagine any of the other candidates for governor working in the hot August sun?"

Carl Sanders became "Cuff Links Carl." (Carter supporters have pointed out that the name was actually coined by one of the Republican candidates; but whether Carter invented it or not, it is representative of the type of attack he launched against the former governor.) Specifically, Carter accused Sanders of having used his office for personal gain. He called on Sanders to make a public financial statement — something Sanders refused to do until it was too late — and at one point produced a sheaf of documentation showing that as governor Sanders had been involved in the financial manipulations of a large corporation. The documents showed that Sanders had served as secretary of Fuqua Industries while governor. This was true, but Sanders denied profiting from the association because he said he hadn't owned any stock.

These tactics worked. When the survey was made in September, 1969, only one percent of the voters believed Sanders had used his office for personal gain; by the time of the primary, the majority of the electorate were convinced of this. Sanders didn't help his own case much with TV spots showing him jogging and boating — the leisure activities of a rich man.

Throughout the campaign there was a running battle between Carter and the Atlanta press, who backed Sanders. Of this war Carter has written in his autobiography:

> My biggest problem and worst mistake invovled one of the Atlanta newspapers. The editor [Reg Murphy] early in the campaign began to characterize me as an ignorant and bigoted redneck peanut farmer. Editorial cartoons showed me standing in the muck of racism while all the other candidates disappeared into the sunrise of enlightenment. These attacks had a serious effect on some of our tentatively - committed, liberal, and idealistic supporters who did not know me personally, particularly those in the Atlanta area who might have helped us financially. . . .
>
> I wrote an ill-tempered letter attacking the newspaper, but it was not published. When all the candidates were invited to address the annual convention of the Georgia Press Association, I used my time on the program to read the letter to all the state's editors. It was a mistaken and counterproductive action.[5]

Carter may not have been at ease in the role of press hater. Nevertheless, it did win him votes because in the mind of the average voter the Atlanta press and the establishment were synonymous. Afterwards, Bill Pope, who worked on the Carter campaign, said, "We loved all those scurrilous cartoons. We just didn't want it to stop."

Another factor behind Carter's victory over Sanders was the tremendous amount of personal campaigning he put in. Hamilton had advised that "Carter should concentrate heavily on the working man, both the skilled and the unskilled," and this was exactly what he did. Bill Shipp describes the new direction Carter's campaign took thus:

> Carter had spent the previous two years on the chicken-and-peas civic club speech-making circuit. The poll showed it had not helped him much.
>
> He later passed up the Civitan and Rotary speeches in favor of shaking hands at factory gates and rubbing shoulders with the good old boys around service stations and garages all over the state.
>
> The factory foremen ran him away from their gates. The workers looked at him as if he were trying to sell them something they didn't want to buy.
>
> But he and his wife, Rosalynn, and his mother, Mrs. Lillian Carter, 72, persisted. They were there at dawn and at midnight, handing out pamphlets (when the factory officials would let them) and looking as if they didn't have a friend in the world. All three often campaigned nonstop from 6 a.m. to midnight six days a week.[6]

Carter went where the people were — to the factories, restaurants, barber shops, beauty parlors, shopping centers, and football games. He shook every hand he could find including one belonging to a mannequin at a department store. Realizing his mistake, he simply turned to an aide and instructed, "Give her a brochure." He also combed the small rural hamlets of the state, where sometimes the people had never seen a gubernatorial candidate before. And everywhere he and his backers went they made people feel that their vote was crucial. Gulliver and Murphy cite the example of Gooseneck County, where a Carter staffer, having failed to get the support of the local powers-that-be, turned to half a dozen young ladies and asked them to serve as precinct captains. "We've always put a lot of store by the Gooseneck Precinct," he told them. "We've always believed that, as goes Gooseneck, so goes Georgia." Apparently, the young ladies of Gooseneck took up the challenge because Carter carried the 30-voter precinct by a margin of 27 to 3.[7]

It was a low-budget campaign, run largely by amateurs, but it was highly effective. As Carter describes it,

> We learned about scheduling, living off the land, and using maximum free news media coverage to supplement good paid advertising . . .
> Neither we nor our staff workers stayed in hotels or motels for which we had to pay. We lived with supporters all over the state, and the late night visits did more than anything else to cement permanent friendships — and to let an effective exchange of information take place between campaign headquarters and people in the individual communities of Georgia. We personally visited the isolated country radio stations, many of which had to operate with a staff of only one or two persons. When we showed up at the station, they almost always welcomed a live or taped interview.[8]

Many who watched Carter campaigning at this time observed how well he came across on a one-to-one basis. No other candidate — except perhaps Lester Maddox — seemed to have the capacity to turn voters on in the way that Carter did.

Sanders' campaign was a very different affair. It involved money, organization, and slick advertising. Also, since he was confident of victory, Sanders didn't bother to stump as Carter did. He simply had signs put up that stated rather flatly that "Carl ought to be elected governor."

But in the final analysis, it was probably the racial issue that was the deciding factor in the contest between Carter and Sanders. Did Carter then, as his critics charge, run a racist campaign in order to win? Gulliver and Murphy see it this way:

It was not that Carter made overtly racist statements, because he did not, and he and his supporters were very sensitive to any charge of racism. But voters in the South have become accustomed to code words, to fine points of approach, in dealing with race as an issue. Carter, for example, spoke sympathetically of Alabama Governor George Wallace and criticized Sanders for having once barred Wallace from a scheduled speaking engagement in Georgia (by refusing to permit the use of a state building for the speech). "I expect to have particularly strong support from the people who voted for George Wallace for president and the ones who voted for Lester Maddox," he said, in an interview early in the summer. Then, in the next breath, he noted that he had "excellent support" among the leadership of the NAACP and Negro churchmen across the state. The remarkable thing was that probably both statements were true. They were diminishingly true as the campaign neared an end. Some Negro spokesmen, notably Dr. Horace Tate, the unsuccessful black candidate for mayor of Atlanta in 1969, remained staunch Carter boosters. Most black voters came to see their choice, however, as between Sanders and King. Most white segregationist voters, those tending to vote for Wallace and Maddox, moved increasingly toward Carter.[9]

Several events were responsible for this polarization of voters. One was the reproduction and distribution of a photograph that was quite innocent when it first appeared, but, in the context of the political campaign, proved harmful to Sanders. It showed him in the dressing room of the Atlantic Hawks basketball team, being doused with champagne during a victory celebration by a black player (Sanders was one of the owners of the team). Thousands of copies of the photograph were mailed anonymously to white Baptist preachers, lawmen, and white barbershops across the state. (This was an old Southern political trick: When you wanted to discredit your opponent, you showed him with a Negro. In one of his campaigns for governor, Gene Talmadge hired a man who closely resembled his opponent, and had him drive around the state in the company of two cigar-puffing Negroes.) Who was responsible? Political writer Steven Brill produced evidence that the Carter campaign was involved.[10] According to Brill, Ray Abernathy, an Atlanta public-relations man who worked with Carter's own ad man, Gerald Rafshoon, stated that Carter backers — specifically, Hamilton Jordan, his '76 campaign manager — took part in the mailing. Carter supporters dismissed the leaflet as "a piece of trivia," and maintained that if it was distributed by anyone in the campaign, it was done by an "overeager supporter" without Carter's knowledge or approval. Abernathy, however, stood by his original allegation. Abernathy also charged that the Carter campaign secretly financed commercials for the black candidate, C. B. King, with the hope of drawing black voters away from Sanders.

Then there was the fact that Carter received the en-

dorsement of two arch-segregationists, former Governor
Marvin Griffin and Roy Harris, editor of the *Augusta
Courier*, a distinctly racist newspaper. Both were bitter
enemies of Sanders and apparently viewed Carter as the
lesser of two evils. Interestingly enough, J. B. Stoner,
the racist candidate mentioned earlier, thought that Griffin was "crazy" to back Carter because according to
Stoner, Carter was "the biggest race mixer in the race for
governor." He even called the *Atlanta Constitution* to
say so.

In the case of Roy Harris, Carter found himself in a
somewhat embarrassing position. After a speech at one
university campus, he was asked by a student if as governor he would reappoint Roy Harris, who was on the state
Board of Regents and was extremely unpopular with
students. Carter said "no." Perhaps he wanted to show
the students, who had become increasingly critical of him
since 1966 when they had supported him, that he was still
the "good guy" of four years earlier. In any event, he later
denied that he had said he wouldn't reappoint Roy Harris.
What he had really meant, he said, was that he had no
intention of appointing or reappointing anyone at the time
(as governor he did not reappoint Roy Harris to the Board
of Regents). The incident points up the dilemma Carter
faced in his attempts to reconcile his former liberal supporters with his new friends, the Wallace people.

Another issue upon which he seemed to take conflicting
positions was that of private schools. Many of these
schools were established in the wake of federal desegre-
gation legislation. Early in the campaign, Carter denounced them as "fly-by-night," saying that he was "not
in favor of putting a single dime of taxpayers' money in

private schools." Later on in the campaign, however, he
visited a private school in the Piedmont region of Georgia
and told backers from 13 South Georgia counties at a rally
in Tifton not to "let anybody, including the Atlanta newspapers, mislead you into criticizing private education."
Why did Carter shift ground in this case? Charles Kirbo,
one of Carter's top political advisors, offered an explanation. He said that there were some good people involved
with private schools; that they weren't all founded for
racist reasons; and that these people came to Carter and
complained that he was grouping them all together in one
bag (he had apparently been advised earlier not to take a
stand on the question of private schools).[11]

Carter's staff also advised him not to campaign in black
communities, something which he did anyway. Reporters
covering the candidates noted that while some only shook
hands with whites, Carter made a point of shaking hands
with everyone — black and white. Presumably, Carter's
staff didn't think he should bother with blacks because
they were going to vote for Sanders or C. B. King, anyway. Yet one can't help wondering if a fear of alienating
the Wallace vote wasn't involved, too. Carter's mother,
who was well known for her liberal attitudes on race,
remarked that she had to watch what she said during the
1970 campaign. Her statement leads to further speculation as to just how far Carter could afford to go without
treading too heavily on the toes of the Wallacites. He did
say throughout his campaign that if elected he would
appoint qualified blacks to high-level constitutional positions, where they had never served before. But the segregationists voted for him anyway, so either they didn't
believe him or simply chose to ignore what he said.
Charles Kirbo feels that Carter was able to appeal to the

working people of the state on questions other than race, such as jobs, food, and housing. "Jimmy knows enough about people that he can get them to vote for him even when they disagree with him," Kirbo says.

There's no doubt that during the 1970 race Jimmy Carter showed himself to be a very astute politician. As Gulliver and Murphy have pointed out, code words are important in Southern politics, especially in terms of the racial issue. Take the words *liberal* and *conservative*, for instance. In Georgia and in most of the other Southern states, these words have racial connotations. *Liberal* means liberal on racial matters, while *conservative* generally means segregationist. While he was running for governor and after he was elected, Carter denied being a liberal. "I don't consider myself a liberal," he emphasized. "One of the standard speeches I made [during the campaign] — I know it by heart — is that Georgia people are conservative, but their conservatism does not mean racism . . . that we hide our heads in the sand and refuse to recognize that changes are inevitable in a fast-changing technological society . . . that we are callous or unconcerned about our fellow man . . . Georgians are conservative. So am I."[12] Carter ran as a conservative, but in the process changed the meaning of the term. He created his own code; most Georgians, however, already had another.

In the Democratic primary Carter polled only 5% of the black vote. Nevertheless, enough "conservatives" voted for him to enable him to come out ahead of Sanders, though without a clear majority. At this point Sanders rolled up his sleeves and launched an attack on Carter. He accused Carter of being a "slaver" and a "slum landlord," and an atheist as well. (This latter charge was based on the fact that as a state senator Carter had voted against a constitutional amendment that would have required God to be worshipped in Georgia.) Sanders also finally released a financial statement. But it was too late. In the run-off Carter defeated him.

Interviewed after the election, Sanders complained, "I was frozen in. Everybody knew what I was and what I stood for. I couldn't get out there on the streets in June and start waving my arms and saying, 'Hooray for George Wallace.' People knew me too well for that. It wouldn't have worked."[13]

A Carter aide had this comment on the result: "Remember the Edsel. Carl Sanders was the Edsel in this campaign. The advertising brought the traffic to the showroom, but they didn't buy. The advertising also brought traffic into our store. The people liked Carter and they bought. He was the right product at the right time. All the advertising did was make him better known."[14] And referring back to the poll which had originally shown Carter how he could beat Sanders, Gerald Rafshoon, Carter's ad man, said, "Any smart leader, anybody who wants to be governor, should listen to good technical advice. If he doesn't, then he isn't qualified to be governor. Sears would not go into a multi-million-dollar promotion without getting some research done on what the people want to buy."[15] The product that most Georgians wanted to buy in the election year of 1970 was apparently one that had just enough of a hint of racism.

But this didn't necessarily mean that Carter himself was a racist. As Atlanta Senator Leroy Johnson, a black who supported Sanders in the primary, put it:

He [Carter] is going to be one of the greatest governors this state has ever had. I served with him in the Senate, you know. I knew he wasn't a racist then. And I know now that he is going to do more for blacks than any governor has ever done. We'll have some black judges appointed by Jimmy Carter. Just wait and see . . . He has the genuine desire to right a lot of wrongs . . . I understand why he ran that kind of ultraconservative campaign . . . you have to do that to win. And that's the main thing. I don't believe you can win this state without being a racist. Five years from now, perhaps — but not now.[16]

Having defeated Sanders, Carter found himself on the Democratic ticket with his former opponent, Lester Maddox, who was now running for lieutenant governor. (Under Georgia law a governor cannot succeed himself.) Prior to the general election, Carter spoke warmly of his running mate. He said that Maddox had brought a "high standard of forthright expression and personal honesty to the governor's office." Maddox, on his part, kept his distance. He warned Carter to stick to his campaign promises — "When I put my money in a peanut machine, I don't expect to get bubble gum." He also told him that he had better not interfere with the control of the senate Maddox expected to exercise as lieutenant governor. Once in office the two men would bitterly oppose each other, but for the moment Carter felt he had to back his running mate.

In the general election, Carter easily defeated his Republican opponent, Hal Suit, a TV newscaster and newcomer to politics. Carter received 60% of the vote; Maddox did even better with 73%. These results were no surprise to anyone. In October before the election, the Republicans had had a professional poll taken that showed that Suit might as well write off the election unless he could manage to top Carter's lead in South Georgia, described as "the power base of the State's most raucous political practitioners — Tom Watson, Eugene Talmadge, Herman Talmadge, and now, Lester Maddox." South Georgians had turned out overwhelmingly for Wallace in 1968, and now they were backing Carter. The poll showed Carter as winning three-fourths of the potential Wallace vote, and "this Carter-Wallace segment is apparently Carter's most dedicated and loyal source of support."[17] Thus it was clear that Carter needed the Wallace vote just as much in November as he had in September against Carl Sanders. As one long-time observer of the political scene would comment later on, "Carter has the knack of seeing things clearly that are necessary. Wallace and Maddox were heroes and Carter had sense enough to see it."[18]

Jimmy Carter was sworn in as the state's seventy-sixth governor on January 12, 1971. It had been a long and often difficult road from Plains to the state capitol. Behind him was a campaign for which he wasn't going to get any "nice guy" of the year awards. However, as he had learned in 1966, being nice and good aren't always enough to win. Four years later he took a hard look at political realities and mapped his strategy accordingly.

The 1970 campaign was a dirty one, but then Carter certainly didn't set any new records in this respect. All gubernatorial campaigns in the state are dirty, a Georgian said recently; and went on to characterize Southern politics in general as "go for the throat."

Questioned about the campaign six years later during his presidential bid, Carter would say, "If you ever find one instance in the 1970 campaign where I ever insinuated anything about race or tried to make people think I was a racist, you know I will admit it on the front porch of The Washington Post building in Washington."[19] And a man who had watched Carter's rise would comment, "That's Jimmy. He's one of the most cocksure men I've ever encountered in public life. Unlike Lot's wife, he never casts his eye backward."[20]

No, Jimmy Carter wasn't looking backward as he stood on the steps of the capitol that January morning. Instead he was looking forward — to the term as governor that lay ahead of him.

Columbus Ledger-Enquirer

CHAPTER 5

South Georgia Turtle for Governor

As secretary of state for over 30 years, Ben Fortson had seen a lot of Georgia governors come and go — Ernest Vandiver, Marvin Griffin, Carl Sanders, Lester Maddox — to name a few. Now Jimmy Carter was chief executive. Carter was no stranger to Fortson; they were both from South Georgia, and a relative of his, Warren Fortson, had helped Carter in his battle over the election fraud in Quitman County in 1962. Ben Fortson had kept an eye on Carter during his two terms as state senator, and had watched him campaign in 1966 and 1970. He felt he knew the man. The state legislature apparently thought he did too because they called on Fortson with some questions about Carter. Specifically, they wanted to know if Carter was really serious about his plans for reorganizing state government. "He's serious, all right," Fortson told them. He went on to compare Carter to a South Georgia turtle, a pretty stubborn critter. When a South Georgia turtle meets an obstacle in its path, it doesn't go around it; instead the turtle just keeps pushing and pushing until the obstacle is removed.

During his four-year term as governor, Jimmy Carter

constantly encountered obstacles in his path, but, as Fortson had predicted, he just kept pushing until eventually, though not always, he got what he wanted.

The major thrusts of Carter's administration were spelled out in his inaugural address, delivered January 12, 1971. At this time he said, "Our people are our most precious possession and we cannot afford to waste the talents and abilities given by God to one single Georgian. Every adult illiterate, every school dropout, every untrained retarded child is an indictment of us all. Our state pays a terrible and continuing human financial price for these failures. It is time to end this waste. If Switzerland and Israel and other people can eliminate illiteracy, then so can we. The responsibility is our own, and as Governor, I will not shirk this responsibility." But this was not all. Carter went on to make history with the statement, "I say to you quite frankly that the time for racial discrimination is over. Our people have already made this major and difficult decision, but we cannot underestimate the challenge of hundreds of minor decisions yet to be made. Our inherent human charity and our religious beliefs will be taxed to the limit. No poor, rural, weak, or black person should ever have to bear the additional burden of being deprived of the opportunity of an education, a job, or simple justice." One can only imagine the thoughts of Carter's segregationist lieutenant governor as he stood next to Carter and listened to these words. Was this the man that the supporters of Lester Maddox and George Wallace had put into office?

Carter pledged that his administration would serve the people of the state through better social programs; he also expressed concern for the environment: "Georgia is a state of great natural beauty and promise, but the quality of our natural surroundings is threatened because of avarice, selfishness, procrastination and neglect. Change and development are necessary for the growth of our population and for the progress of our agricultural, recreational, and industrial life. Our challenge is to insure that such activities avoid destruction and dereliction of our environment. The responsibility for meeting this challenge is our own. As governor, I will not shirk this responsibility."

At the same time as he expressed the goals of his administration, Carter made it clear how he meant to govern. He said, "We should remember that our state can best be served by a strong and independent governor, working with a strong and independent legislature." He continued: "Here seated around me are the members of the Georgia legislature and other state officials. They are dedicated and honest men and women. They love this state as you love it and I love it. But no group of elected officials, no matter how dedicated or enlightened, can control the destiny of a great state like ours. What officials can solve alone the problems of crime, welfare, illiteracy, disease, injustice, pollution, and waste? This control rests in *your* hands, the people of Georgia."

Carter did not say it here, but he believed that only the governor could speak with one voice for the people. They were his ace in the hole in the many gambles he undertook during his administration. Like another South Georgia politician before him, Carter understood that as long as he had the people behind him he could do whatever he wanted. Once when Gene Talmadge as commissioner of agriculture faced impeachment charges for losing $10,000 of the state's money in a hog-price-pegging deal, he was able to raise enough popular support to get a petition signed demanding that the proceedings against him be dropped. Afterwards, he announced to his delighted supporters, "Sure I stole. But I stole it for you." They loved him for saying that.

Carter had a much higher regard for the people than Talmadge; and unlike the Wild Man of Sugar Hill, he honestly tried to do his best by them. But still he needed their support, and here from the very beginning of his administration he faced certain problems. The minute he declared that, "The time for racial discrimination is over," he began to get a great deal of national publicity as a liberal, and the rednecks who had voted for him began to wonder if they hadn't made a serious mistake. Carter had to convince them that he was still one of them. The skillful manner in which he managed to do this comes out clearly in his handling of the Lt. Calley incident.

Lt. William Calley's trial took place in Georgia where there was a great deal of sentiment against the proceedings and against Calley's ultimate conviction. Several local draft board heads resigned in protest; Lester Maddox appealed to President Nixon to free Calley; and the state commander of the Veterans of Foreign Wars called on Carter as governor to declare a day of mourning for Calley. With the protest mounting, Carter took all the calls relating to the Calley case personally. Then on April 2, 1971, he called a news conference in which he said that he was impressed with "the responsible attitude taken by Georgians" in this matter. He expressed concern that persons both within the country and without "would use these events to further their own ambition, to cheapen and shame the reputation of American servicemen, and to shake the faith of Americans in their country." He said that Calley was a "scapegoat" and that his superiors should have received the same treatment. He did not, as many of his supporters wanted, proclaim William Calley Day, but rather "American Fighting Men's Day," in which Georgians were asked to demonstrate their "complete support for our servicemen, concern for our country, and rededication to the principles which made our country great."

Later questioned about the Calley incident during the 1976 presidential campaign, Carter would say, "I never thought Calley was anything but guilty. I never felt any attitude toward Calley except abhorrence. And I thought he should be punished and still do. I never expressed any contrary opinion."[1] Yet whatever Carter's personal feelings may have been, they were not explicitly expressed in his public statement. He did not want to offend the many Georgians who were behind Calley, so he purposely spoke in very general terms and did not specifically condemn Calley's action in the My Lai Massacre. To have done so would have simply added fuel to the fire. It also would have cost him the support of many who had originally voted for him. As Bill Shipp, associate editor of the *Atlanta Constitution* saw it, Carter "must practice just enough Georgia-brand demogogery to keep the natives from getting so restless that his programs will be wrecked."[2]

At the time of the Calley episode, the program that Carter was especially concerned about was his plan to reorganize the state government. Governmental reorganization had been a part of Carter's platform when he was campaigning for governor. Then he thought there were 140 governmental agencies. Once in office, however, he discovered that there were over 200. "It's gotten so that every time I open the closet door in my office, I fear a new state agency will fall out," he joked in his State of the State Address. Nevertheless, he was deadly serious about doing something about the situation. The last time the state government had been reorganized was in 1931 when Governor Richard B. Russell had cut the number of state agencies from 107 to 18, saving taxpayers millions of dollars. Over the years, however, state agencies had proliferated, often without rhyme or reason. There were, for example, 36 different agencies dealing with natural resources. Through a streamlining of the government, Carter hoped, like Russell, to save money by eliminating waste and inefficiency. He also hoped to improve the delivery of services to the people.

The idea of reorganization did not originate with Carter. Several states had recently streamlined their governments, and in Georgia under Carl Sander's administration a beginning was made in this direction. The Governor's Commission for Efficiency and Improvement had made recommendations for administrative reform, but no overall program had been accepted by the legislature. There were just too many people in government who felt they stood to lose through reorganization. Thus it was risky business for Carter to make it an issue and, more than that, to stake the success of his administration on the enactment of his reorganization plan. If he couldn't get this main piece of legislation through, he would certainly lose face with the legislature, and in all likelihood would meet strong opposition to other bills he put forward.

The time had passed when a governor of Georgia had only to suggest to the legislature what he wanted done and have its members fall all over themselves to do it. In particular, the administration of Carter's predecessor, Lester Maddox, had witnessed the rapid development of the legislature into a very independent body, jealous of its powers. Maddox knew little about governing, and was also more interested in getting publicity than he was in actual administration. Thus the legislature was left to do pretty much as it pleased.

Unlike Maddox, Carter was extremely knowledgeable about state government. He had served for two terms in the state legislature, and during the four years between gubernatorial campaigns he had studied Georgia government in such minute detail that he was much better acquainted with it than most new governors. He was also determined to exercise his power as an executive. He was bound to clash with the newly independent legislature and also with Lester Maddox, who was ready to oppose him at every turn. The uneasy truce that had existed while they were running mates had rapidly given way to open warfare. Maddox never forgave Carter for stating in his inaugural address that the time for racial discrimination was over. As one state official was to observe later, "If a man was obnoxious to another, it was Lester to Jimmy Carter." In addition to the Maddox crowd in the senate, Carter faced the opposition of disgruntled Sanders' supporters, who were eager for an opportunity to embarrass him politically. The stage was set for the first and most important battle of Carter's administration — the fight to pass his government reorganization plan.

It was a big gamble, but through a rather brilliant tactical maneuver, Carter managed to stack the deck in his favor. What he won from the first legislative session was the authorization to go ahead with the planning aspect of reorganization. He could, of course, have gone ahead anyway, but then he would have faced serious problems in obtaining the legislature's final approval of his plan. He proposed and got a kind of reverse veto (since traditionally the veto power is the prerogative of the executive rather than the legislature), whereby the reorganization plan that was developed would automatically become law 15 days after the beginning of the next legislative session, unless vetoed by a majority in the house and the senate. The burden of defeating the plan was placed on its opponents, who were faced with the task of mustering a majority of negative votes. The vote giving Carter this authority was a close one, but Carter managed to squeak by with one vote to spare.

The next step involved the actual reorganization planning. For this Carter assembled a staff of over 100 state employees, volunteers from business and labor, and four members of a management consulting firm. The staff worked long hours, under tremendous pressure, because of tight deadlines, analyzing every aspect of state government. Carter worked very closely with the staff, becoming as involved in every detail of the plan as the staff was. When it was finally completed, the proposal very definitely bore his mark.

The reorganization staff made 300 recommendations, 90% of which were ultimately accepted, but not without a fight. Maddox blasted the plan as an attempt by Carter to set up a dictatorship. The Georgia Medical Association was up in arms because the State Board of Health was to be abolished, and the reorganized Health Department was to have a lay-dominated board. Many public officials felt that Carter was simply trying to do too much too fast. As one Georgian was later to remark, "With government reorganization Jimmy stepped into a lot of people's private briar patches."

There were no more jokes about state agencies coming out of the woodwork in Carter's second State of the State Address. Instead he confronted the opposition head-on:

> We should not be misled by highly publicized opposition to reorganization. Although most news media have tried to be objective and fair, there have been distortions.
>
> Let me point out to you that there is no division in purpose between me as governor and you as legislators. You are my people. Governors do not pass laws — *you* have given me an overwhelming mandate in House Bill #1 (the original "enabling" legislation) to reform the executive branch of government. For a year now I have been carrying out that mandate.
>
> Opposition is the same as it was a year ago, when a very small number of legislators joined with a few department heads and board members and attempted to block this effort . . . How much have you heard about the state department heads who have worked throughout the year in a completely dedicated way and now await the benefits to be derived from this comprehensive and far-reaching plan? . . . How much have you read about the dozens of medical doctors and psychiatrists in private practice, the psychologists, nurses, social workers, nursing home directors, bankers, voca-

tional rehabilitation counselors, conservationists, civic
clubs, grand juries, jaycees and women's clubs who
have endorsed this effort?

Most importantly, how much have you read about
the thousands of Georgians who are not organized to
represent a particular interest, but who are merely
confused, frustrated, and even alienated from our government because of its complexity, inefficiency, and
inability to meet their legitimate demands?

The future of Georgia depends on continued cooperation between the governor and the General Assembly.

Many criticisms of Carter for his unwillingness to
compromise stemmed from the reorganization battle.
Hamilton Jordan, who was then his executive secretary,
recalled that, "Once some legislator wanted a promotion
for his father-in-law. We needed his vote, so we asked
Jimmy to do it. He said he didn't spend four years of his
life running for governor to promote some guy's father-
in-law. He wouldn't do it — and here we were, idealistic
young kids, urging *him* to be more political.[3]

Carter did use some strong-arm tactics to bring legislators around to his way of thinking, but he was capable of
gentler methods of persuasion as well. At breakfast,
lunch, and dinner he met with various legislators, coaxing
and even "preaching to them." He also took his case
directly to the people. The Citizen's Committee for Reorganization, consisting of staffers from Carter's '70 campaign, mailed out hundreds of handbills explaining the
reorganization plan and calling on citizens to put pressure
on their state legislators to support it.

In the end Carter won, again by a very close vote.

Reorganization was implemented. Yet when the smoke of battle had cleared, there were questions as to how much reorganization had actually taken place and whether or not the plan accomplished all that it was supposed to.

Reorganization involved structural changes and management improvements. In terms of structure, the number of agencies was reduced, and those with like functions were grouped together. Thus some thirty agencies dealing with such areas as game and fish, environmental and land-use questions were merged to form a Department of Natural Resources; the state Highway Department gave way to a new Department of Transportation, covering all modes of transportation; and 21,000 employees in welfare and health agencies were brought together in one giant Department of Human Resources, and so on. Exactly how many agencies were eliminated? Carter claimed to have cut the number of agencies from 300 to 22, but in actual fact there were only 65 *budgeted* agencies when he started out. He also claimed to have eliminated 2,100 unnecessary state jobs, but State Auditor Ernest Davis pointed out that these jobs existed only on paper. No jobs were eliminated, and the number of state employees increased from 34,322 to 42,000 during Carter's term in office.

When Gene Talmadge wanted to cut the cost of state government, he simply fired everyone in sight. But Carter was not about to do this. As James T. Wooten of the *New York Times* expressed it: ". . . Confronted by a bureaucracy weighted by decades of patronage and populated by thousands of men and women whose jobs represented the difference between survival and unemployment, he [Carter] tempered his hard-line attitude on efficiency and compromised on wholesale job cuts that would have saved millions of dollars and perhaps contributed to a much more efficient government. . . ."[4]

Critics of reorganization also questioned whether it was better to have a small number of large agencies rather than a large number of small ones. They pointed to the massive foul-ups resulting from the centralization of the state computer system. The Department of Human Resources was another target of attack. Carter was determined to have a "single-door" approach to all health, welfare, and related social services, but the DHR proved too huge to be administered effectively. As someone said, trying to get a hold on DHR was like wrestling a hippopotamus in a swimming pool of glue. Carter himself realized that there were problems with DHR but hoped that in time they could be worked out. His successor, Governor George Busbee, was authorized by the legislature to make changes, but said that he would not break it up, as some of Carter's opponents urged.

The management improvements, which came with reorganization, included changes in budgeting and investment policies. Zero-based budgeting was instituted. This meant that in theory every program had to justify its existence on a yearly basis. However, as it actually worked out on the state level, operations were broken down into "decision packages" with the various department heads assigning priorities. Zero-based budgeting did give Carter a good handle on how state monies were being spent, but State Auditor Ernest Davis said that agency heads were able to get around the system by assigning low priorities to things that they knew had so much popular support that they couldn't be done away with and high priorities to things that didn't have as much popular support.

However, there is little dispute that investment policies were changed for the better during Carter's administration. Previously, "idle" state funds had been deposited in low interest-bearing bank accounts. Carter offered to deposit this money by public bids to any Georgia bank and thus obtained higher interest rates. He boosted the state's income significantly from these accounts. In addition, through a computer-controlled "cash flow" system, he made certain that as state funds became available, they were deposited in interest-bearing accounts.

Still, the big question for many people was whether or not reorganization saved money. Carter claimed to have saved the state $50 million a year, but this figure is a matter of dispute. It is difficult to document because it has to do with cuts in projected spending increases rather that actual budget decreases. During Carter's administration the state budget increased by 58.5 percent from $1,057 million to $1,675 million. (This was less than the 61% increase under Maddox's administration, but more than the increase in the Consumer Price Index for the period, which showed a nationwide jump of 38.1 percent.) Carter could have saved by cutting back on the budget, as Gene Talmadge, for example, had done. But Carter had too strong a commitment to social programs, corrections, and the preservation of the environment — all things which cost a great deal of money.

In Georgia today there is a definite lack of consensus as to the success of reorganization. Some feel it should never have been done, that it created more problems than solutions; others believe that it was necessary and that it did improve the delivery of government services to the people of the state; still others think it is too soon to judge the effectiveness of reorganization. In a paper entitled "Georgia State Administration: Jimmy Carter's Contribution," political scientist T. McN. Simpson concluded:

> There is no question that reorganization, in both its two chief senses [structural reform and management improvement] has had its costs and will continue to have costs as well as benefits. Those who have been hurt or inconvenienced have naturally reacted, and their reactions, coupled to other influences, have led to some exaggeration of the amount of reorganization which has actually taken place. Particularly in the structural sense, changes, except in a few departments, have been modest. The executive branch has been somewhat simplified and clarified, and the Governor's powers have been slightly enlarged. That "reorganization" has come to be exaggerated by its proponents as well as its opponents does not alter the fact that reorganization has been significant. Modification of governmental structure is an important, if often unattended, phase of public administration, and it is to Governor Carter's credit that he did not take the structure he acquired as already perfect to its tasks.[5]

At the same time as the much-publicized government reorganization was going on, steps were also being taken to reorganize the state's judicial system. In his inaugural address Carter had said that "No poor, rural, weak, or black person should ever have to bear the additional burden of being deprived of the opportunity of an education, a job, or simple justice." The last part of this statement implied a recognition of the need for judicial reform. Thus in 1971 Carter established the Governor's Commission on Judicial Processes to make recommendations for improvements. Instead of proposing a comprehensive program of reform — a method which had failed in the past — the commission submitted thirty recommended changes to be considered separately. Most of these recommendations were eventually implemented through legislative action, through constitutional amendments, through executive order, or administratively. These reform measures included the establishment of a unified court system, a merit system for the selection of judges, and a constitutional means for the discipline and removal of judges. All in all, these changes represented a considerable advance over the past system.

In the area of prison reform, Carter didn't solve all the problems, as he himself would be the first to admit, but he did make a start. Carter persuaded Ellis MacDougal, a nationally known penal system reformer, to come to Georgia and serve as the head of the newly created Department of Offender Rehabilitation. Although the actual number of inmates didn't decrease during Carter's term, substantial progress was made in developing rehabilitative programs, which had been sadly lacking in the past. To help ease the overcrowded situation in the prisons, community correctional centers, housing 400 to 500 inmates each, were set up.

Carter used a similar approach in the field of mental health. Here a "cure-oriented" man was put in charge of the program. As a result many mentally retarded patients were taken out of the overcrowded state institution at Milledgeville and sent to newly created local centers. At these centers retarded children are taught basic skills by nonprofessional staff under the supervision of trained professionals. The program was opposed by a powerful senator who apparently felt that mental patients should remain locked up in the state institution, which could do little more than feed them. However, Carter successfully defended the new "open door" policy.

With regard to drug addicts and alcoholics, the emphasis was also on rehabilitation. By executive order Carter created the Georgia Narcotics Program to provide treatment and rehabilitation for drug addicts. Alcoholism was removed from the realm of a criminal offense by legislative action, and alcoholics were given treatment through the state health services.

In the health field, a "Killers and Cripplers" program to deal with problems of inadequate maternal and infant care, stroke prevention and screening, crippled children, and alcoholism was established. A sickle-cell anemia screening program was started and existing family planning facilities were improved.

As for education, an Adequate Program for Education Law was passed, which provided for such things as preschool education for every child, reduction of pupil-teacher ratios, increases in the number of vocational education teachers, and the equalization of the quality of education throughout the state by providing for more state funds to less wealthy school systems. Preschool education, special education, and vocational education were specific areas receiving special attention. Also, for the first time state funds were used in the construction of public libraries.

Carter's record in environmental protection was a strong one. (On the basis of this record, the League of Conservation Voters would rate Carter, along with Morris Udall, as an "outstanding prospect for president"; ratings of other '76 candidates ranged from "fair" to "hopeless.") In his autobiography Carter states that, with the exception of reorganization, he spent more time working to preserve natural resources than on any other single issue. During his term as governor, spending on natural resources rose from $55 million a year to $70 million. He created a Heritage Trust Commission to preserve and restore natural and historic areas, and successfully bucked the U.S. Army Corps of Engineers in their efforts to construct an unnecessary dam on Georgia's scenic Flint River. He also pushed for and got tighter air and water pollution controls, and was one of the loudest protestors among the various governors when President Nixon impounded federal pollution control grants. He insisted that new industries planning to move into the state demonstrate that they would be able to meet the state's antipollution regulations. He also took a stand against lobbyists from the strip-mining industry, who were seeking more favorable legislation.

In the area of race relations, Leroy Johnson was proven right in his prediction that Carter would do more for blacks in the state than any governor before him. As he had promised during his campaign, Carter appointed blacks to major state boards and agencies, especially those having extensive dealings with black citizens. He put blacks on the Board of Paroles and Pardons, in the state Welfare Department, and on the state Board of Regents. When Carter came into office, there were only three blacks serving on major state boards and agencies; when he left, there were 53. He also increased the number of black state employees from 4,850 to 6,684. However, he appointed only one black judge. He chose a young black patrolman to be one of the four security guards who accompanied him around the state; and once when he got a call not to bring the black security guard with him to a speech at a Macon, Georgia, country club, he did just that and proceeded to give his audience a lecture on race relations. Carter established a Civil Disorder Unit — the first of its kind in any state — consisting of two blacks and two whites to deal with racial disturbances; and a Governor's Council on Human Relations, composed of six black members and six whites, which led to the formation of a statewide association of human relations.

What he did on a symbolic level was important too. For the first time in Georgia, January 15, 1973, was proclaimed Martin Luther King, Jr., Day in honor of the slain civil rights leader; and a year later King's portrait was hung in the state capitol as Carter and an integrated audience sang, "We Shall Overcome," and the Ku Klux Klan staged a demonstration outside.

On the question of busing, Carter took a stand against the forced busing of school children to achieve racial integration. In 1972 white parents in Augusta, Georgia, staged a one-day boycott of the schools in opposition to forced busing. The object of the boycott was to get the state legislature to appeal to Congress to call a constitutional convention to consider an anti-busing amendment. Carter said he would support the boycott as a last resort if the legislature didn't pass such a resolution. (They did.) He called "The massive forced busing of students . . . the most serious threat to education I can remember." He did, however, support the voluntary busing program established in Atlanta. Many blacks also favored the Atlanta plan.

As governor, Carter pushed for "government-in-sunshine" legislation, but the extent of his achievement in this area is a matter of debate. He proposed and the legislature passed a law opening many government meetings to the public and to reporters. This was a revision of the state's previous open-meetings law, and some questioned whether the revisions were actually an improvement. Carter was also largely responsible for the passage of a campaign financial disclosure bill, requiring candidates to make public disclosures of all contributions of $101 or more.

During his term Carter traveled fairly frequently in the United States and abroad. He made visits to Europe, Israel, and several Latin American countries, establishing state offices in a number of countries as part of an effort to boost economic growth in the state. He was successful. While he was governor, economic development grew by $2.5 billion in capital investment, and 89,000 new jobs were created.

Carter had promised property tax relief, and in 1973 he proposed and had passed a bill providing a $50 million rebate to all property taxpayers, not only homeowners and renters. But as evidence tended to show that the bill actually benefited major corporations more than the poor people it was supposed to help, Carter vetoed a proposed continuation of it the next year. In other legislation, he pressed for laws establishing standardized property appraisal methods, and making available a less expensive process of appeal for property owners with grievances.

For all his many legislative victories, Carter also had some defeats. An important one was his failure to secure consumer protection legislation. Carter himself called this his major disappointment. He was opposed by powerful special interest groups, but he also admitted that he started the fight too late in his administration. As a result the state still has the weakest consumer protection laws in the country and is, in Carter's own words, "a dumping ground for con artists, shysters, and unscrupulous businessmen."

There is no doubt that Carter left problems behind him. The state's school dropout rate is still among the highest in the country; Georgia students still do poorly on national scholastic tests; prisons are still overcrowded; pollution continues to foul the environment. The overall picture presented by national statistics did not show significant improvement during Carter's term. In 1970 Georgia was 35th in the country in terms of personal income per person; four years later the state ranked 36th. At the beginning of this period Georgia ranked 48th in average earnings of manufacturing workers; at the end the state ranked 45th. The state also rose from 41st to 37th in terms of public school expenditures.

There were many things that didn't happen as Carter wanted them to, simply because his term ended and the recession set in. Yet, asked the famous Rickover question, "Did you do your best?" shortly before he left office, Jimmy Carter answered with a firm "yes."

In the Rickover tradition, Carter was a hardworking

governor. He never arrived at the capitol later than 7:15 a.m. and often worked late into the night either at his office or at the governor's mansion. Carter's staff found him a rather stern taskmaster who expected staffers to have done their homework and was sparing of praise. The '76 campaign manager, Hamilton Jordan, who served as executive secretary to Carter while he was governor, said, "Jimmy is not easy to get close to. He doesn't have enough time in his life to let people get close. He doesn't understand the personal element in politics, though nobody is better at campaigning."

All those who worked with Carter agreed that he was a tremendously intelligent man. Attorney General Arthur K. Bolton called Carter the smartest man to serve as governor during his lifetime, and Richard B. Cobb, a deputy director of the Office of Planning and Budget, praised Carter for his remarkable capacity for detail. Cobb said that when Carter and the staff were working on the reorganization plan, Carter demonstrated greater familiarity with every aspect of it than did the staff.

Carter gave the state a scandal-free administration. He also set a high standard in terms of his major appointments. During his term high-caliber people were put in charge of such areas as transportation, human resources, and offender rehabilitation.

Nevertheless, Carter made many enemies among fellow politicians because of his refusal to play the usual political games. Those who came to his office to get the favors they felt their support merited were in for a rude surprise, for Carter simply showed them to the door. "Jimmy never rewarded his friends," said one supporter who had sought a position and was turned down. "Instead he looked to the most qualified people." The example is given of John Blackmon, who served as revenue commissioner under Maddox. Traditionally, a new governor selects a new revenue commissioner, but Carter looked at Blackmon, saw he was qualified, and kept him on.

Carter had been elected without the backing of the state Democratic party leaders, and he remained very much of a political loner as governor. Like Talmadge, he depended on his own handpicked entourage rather than political cronies. Hamilton Jordan, a fellow South Georgian who had been youth coordinator of Carter's 1966 campaign and director of the '70 effort, served as executive secretary. Press secretary Jody Powell joined Carter's staff as a driver in the 1970 campaign. Previously he had been a graduate student in political science at Emory University, and before that he attended the Air Force Academy, where he was expelled for cheating on an exam. It was a young staff — both Jordan and Powell were in their late twenties — and an aggressive one, no more tactful in its relations with the legislature than Carter himself. Jody Powell was particularly outspoken in defense of his boss. Once when a woman wrote a letter that was highly critical of Carter, Powell sent her a reply in which he told her to take several big jumps and go straight to hell. His letter aroused some comment when it was printed in one of the Atlanta newspapers, but Carter stood behind his press secretary.

Although he had an extremely dedicated staff, Carter still made his own decisions. "Carter listens," recalled a former aide, "but the ultimate strategy for running a state government or a campaign is his own."

In his dealings with the legislators, Carter did not engage in the usual horse-trading. He would not, for example, offer state roads and other public works in exchange for votes, as had been done in the past. Still, he was capable of withholding his approval from private bills when it was a question of bringing a particular legislator over to his side. On the whole, however, he preferred public confrontation, openly attacking both legislators and lobbyists who opposed his programs. At one point he called the legislature "the worst" in the history of the state; at another, he lashed out against the Georgia Chamber of Commerce, saying it was "one of the most damaging lobbyist groups in the state."

Was he ruthless? "If you're not with him, he'll cut your throat," said one embittered politician. "Sure, he was ruthless," commented a long-time observer of the political scene, "You can't be an effective governor in the South unless you're ruthless." Old Gene (Talmadge), who used methods that were much more extreme than any used by Carter or any other Georgia governor in modern times, once described the problem thus: "A lot of people say they like what I did, but don't like the way I did it. I don't either, but if a bunch of hogs get into your fields or your garden or your flowers and won't come out when you say 'sooey, sooey, sooey,' then you have to use the language and methods that hogs and pigs will understand."

Undoubtedly, Carter was not a compromiser. When convinced he was right (which was most of the time), he refused to bend. Critics charged that this attitude was responsible for his legislative defeats and near-defeats. Carter himself admitted that his inability to compromise was a fault, but didn't feel that, "Georgia suffered under my administration because of it." Carter said he couldn't compromise on matters of principle; others claimed he was just plain mule-headed. State senator Julian Bond said, "I have never seen a man so rigid, and it was not on a question of high principle. Carter just won't give in."[6]

During his term Carter also showed himself to be a highly impatient man. He wanted quick action, and when he didn't get it, he often took matters into his own hands. Thus when the State Board of Health delayed in starting the programs in drug abuse and family planning that he had requested, Carter went ahead and implemented them himself through executive action. He also decided to abolish the State Board of Health, even though the board's chairman was an old college roommate of his and a close friend.

When he couldn't get his way with the legislature, Carter frequently took his case to the people. Yet here he was faced with the problem of selling penny-pinching conservative voters a costly set of liberal social programs. He did this by describing his mental health, education, and prison reforms as examples of good old American business problem-solving. He also presented these programs to the people as examples of Christian charity put into action, at one point going so far as to compare them to Christ's ministry to the suffering. In short, he created a unique political style: "liberalism cloaked in conservative jargon."[7]

Carter's term in office definitely lacked the color of his predecessor, Lester Maddox. He didn't give the people a good show by doing such things as riding a bicycle or a mule backwards. Yet in its legislative accomplishment, Carter's administration reflected "a deep feeling of responsibility for the people, especially the weak and the poor."

Perhaps the best overall characterization of his administration comes from Jimmy Carter himself. In his autobiography he describes it as "highly controversial, aggressive, and combative."

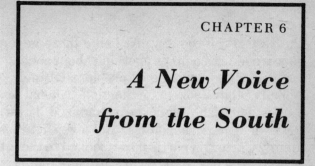

CHAPTER 6

A New Voice from the South

Jimmy Carter's picture on the cover of *Time* magazine? Yes, indeed, there he was on the front of the May 31, 1971, issue. He bore no resemblance to the stereotype of the Southern politician as a jowly, cigar-smoking man, ever ready with a racial slur. Instead Carter appeared young and good looking, a sort of Southern Kennedy. Behind him was a Confederate flag and the caption, "Dixie Whistles a Different Tune." The cover story quoted part of Carter's Inaugural Address, in which he proclaimed that "the time for racial discrimination is over"; and hailed Carter as representative of a new breed of Southern moderate leaders. "The reality of 17 years of court decisions, demonstrations, black-voter registration and legislation was clearly seen across the South as Carter and other moderate governors took office this year. . . ."[1]

Carter and the other governors profiled in *Time* — Linwood Holton of Virginia, John West of South Carolina, Reubin Askew of Florida, and Dale Bumpers of Arkansas — were viewed as the harbingers of a New South, a South freed from the shackles of racism and ready to be accepted once again on an equal footing with the rest of the country. At home these governors were concerned with doing something about solving the social, economic, and educational problems of their states. Nationally, they looked to the time when the South, no longer a pariah, would be recognized as an important force in American politics. But even as these men — Jimmy Carter, in particular — looked to the future, there was still the past to be dealt with, and that race-obsessed past was represented by George Wallace.

Perhaps more than the other governors, Jimmy Carter understood the tremendous appeal of Wallace to many Southerners. Although he had used no stand-in-the-schoolhouse-door rhetoric during his campaign, he had, nevertheless, courted Wallace supporters. To a large extent, he owed his victory to them. His election seemed to indicate that Wallace would probably carry Georgia in 1972. But it opened up other possibilities as well. Hal Gulliver and Reg Murphy offer this analysis of Carter's win in terms of national politics:

> [It] raised a question. Suppose the Democratic presidential nominee were someone Governor Carter could actively support. Could Carter hold former Wallace supporters in the Democratic column in a presidential year?
>
> Carter's own vision of his campaign suggested this possibility. Carter argued, privately, again and again, that many white segregationist-leaning Wallace supporters reacted actually as much from a sense of frustration as from continued racism. Much of this frustration stemmed from the feeling of being pushed around by the federal government, which of course involved racial matters like school desegregation, said Carter.

But, he contended, this sense of alienation from government had come to have a separate life of its own, part of the attitude of many white citizens who, for example, had reconciled themselves to school integration. Carter believed that he could successfully bring such people back into a sense of participation, a relationship to government, without any reference to segregation or racism in any form. His success or failure might determine Wallace's third-party chances in Georgia in 1972.[2]

In public statements after he took office, Carter did express the dissatisfaction of many Southerners with the way the federal government was dealing with the South. He was quoted in the *Atlanta Journal* as saying "I'm tired of being singled out, just because I'm a Southerner, for special rulings by the Supreme Court and federal courts, and special laws passed by Congress and special directives of the present attorney general.

"I think it's time for Georgia people to be treated on an equal basis with all other Americans . . . and I think the other governors feel the same way."[3] And referring specifically to the recent Supreme Court decision on busing, he said that he felt the time had come for the federal government to stop "kicking" the South around.

The upcoming presidential election did, however, offer the possibility for change. Carter and his fellow moderate Southern governors were concerned that the Democratic nominee would be someone that Southerners could support. Together they formed an "unofficial" caucus to be sure that the Democrat's choice would be a man "who doesn't take the South for granted, who doesn't avoid the

South as a political detriment." The South had to be
reckoned with, and all serious Democratic contenders
were advised to take the next plane to Dixie if they
expected Southern backing. Carter also made a point of
inviting Wallace (who might very well have run again as a
third-party candidate in '72) to join with him and other
Southern governors in selecting a Democratic candidate
who would be acceptable to the South. "We share leadership with the same kinds of people," he told the Alabama
governor.

As the Democratic national convention approached,
Carter was critical of the party for "prematurely" ruling
out the possibility of a ticket with Wallace as the vice-
presidential nominee. It was not that he had any great
love for Wallace, but rather that he saw the writing on the
wall in terms of Wallace's popularity in the South. (After
all, Wallace had carried five Southern states in 1968.) In
Carter's view a ticket combining a liberal such as Humphrey with Wallace, who would be certain to win in the
South, could very well lead the Democrats to victory in
November. There is no evidence, however, to suggest
that Carter wanted to see Wallace as his party's presidential nominee. Wallace has charged that Carter reneged on
his promise to nominate him at the convention, but Carter
denies this. He says instead that Wallace asked him if he
would second his nomination at the convention, and that
he refused. Carter's press secretary, Jody Powell, remembers trying to persuade Carter to nominate Wallace.
According to Powell, Carter's response was, "If you want
to get up before the American people and say George
Wallace is qualified to be President, you do it."[4] Carter

chose to nominate another man: Senator Henry "Scoop" Jackson. Carter first met Jackson when he was a young naval officer serving under Admiral Rickover and Jackson was a junior U.S. senator. Like the other Democratic hopefuls, Jackson visited Carter in Georgia, seeking his support. In February, 1972, Carter came very close to publicly endorsing Jackson. At this time he said that Senator Richard Russell had told him to especially keep an eye on Jackson in the next presidential election. Any consideration of personal friendship aside, Jackson was a logical candidate for Carter to support. Whereas McGovern could never be acceptable to the South because of his dovish stand on Vietnam, Jackson's hawkish views gave his candidacy a definite viability with Carter and other Southerners. As Carter saw it, McGovern's nomination would mean that Nixon would carry the South. Thus he joined with organization Democrats and labor in the ABM — Anybody But McGovern — movement. At the convention Humphrey and Muskie withdrew from the race, but Jackson, who earlier had dropped out of the primaries, remained in the running, predicting disaster if McGovern won the nomination. There were many Democrats who shared his view, but by this time most bowed to the inevitability of a McGovern candidacy. Nevertheless, on July 12, 1972, Jimmy Carter stood up in the convention hall and delivered the nominating speech for Scoop Jackson.

Carter's nominating speech is interesting in terms of what it reveals about his thinking at this time. In the very beginning of the speech, he raises the issue of "trust." He says:

In 1960, our people did not understand nor trust big government. They don't trust it now.

In 1960 our people did not trust politicians who were out of touch with the people. They don't trust them now.

In 1960, Americans did not trust those who were tools of special interests, and against the working man, and they don't trust them now.

In short, Americans did not trust Richard Nixon in 1960.

Hundreds of broken promises later their distrust and alienation have been confirmed. Our people know him better now, and they do not trust him today.

In 1960 the Democratic party earned the trust of the American people. How did they earn that trust? By reaching out to the man and the woman in the factories, on the farms, in small businesses, throughout the nation. We earned this trust by letting the ordinary people be an integral part of politics, of government, and public service. . .

We earned the trust and the confidence of the American people in 1960 by nominating a man of compassion and courage. That man was John Fitzgerald Kennedy.

In the above, the word *trust* appears exactly a dozen times, and later on in the speech Carter describes Jackson as "the man who wins elections because the people trust him and because he trusts the people."Carter clearly perceived the importance of winning the trust of the people, and in this perception lay the seeds of his own future presidential campaign. He understood the mood of alienation from government, upon which George Wallace's appeal was based. "We need a man," he said, "who understands that government must be strong and capable in order to protect and serve its people, but that government must always be controlled by the people themselves."

The nominating speech also shows that Carter had Kennedy very much on his mind. In the following paragraphs, for example, he begins with Jackson, but then quickly shifts to Kennedy. He does this so quickly, in fact, that at times it's difficult to tell which man he's talking about:

> In 1970 he [Jackson] beat his last Republican by obtaining 84% of the popular vote. 12 years ago our young Democratic nominee [Kennedy] was an underdog. He had run for vice-president in 1956 and lost. He was a Catholic and many said he could not win because of religious bigotry in this nation. But John Kennedy had faith and he also had sound judgement.
>
> He [back to Jackson again] served as the chairman of our party, this man who understands our people, a man who can bind us together, a man of consistency and truth, a man who has never underestimated the American people. A strong nationwide campaign [back to Kennedy] was mounted and with the help of labor and with the help of farmers and the help of young and with the help of those filled with idealism and hope John Kennedy received his biggest majority in my home state of Georgia. . . .

Carter saw that what the Democrats needed in 1972 was another Kennedy, a man who could bring the diverse elements of the party back together again. McGovern was not the man to do this, and neither — Carter must have realized even as he gave this speech — was Jackson. It was the right speech, but for the wrong man at the wrong time. There was no candidate like Kennedy in 1972, but four years later there would be because Jimmy Carter had decided to run for president in 1976.

Interestingly enough, Carter almost missed the opportunity to give the nominating speech for Jackson because he almost didn't make it to the Democratic convention in Miami. Not because he was ill or otherwise incapacitated, but because a black college student came within 15 votes of being elected as a delegate instead of Carter. Under previous Georgia governors this type of situation could never have arisen because the governors selected both the party's delegates and the members of the state Democratic Executive Committee. In his campaign Carter promised to "democratize" the party, removing control from the bosses and returning it to the people. He kept his promise. As a result the '72 delegates were the first to be elected by the people in the state and Carter almost became the first victim of his own reform. Carter also increased voter participation in the election by deputizing every high school principal in the state as a voting registrar, thus making registration much easier for both blacks and whites.

Meanwhile, back in Miami, McGovern had the nomination, and there was some speculation as to whether he might choose an ABM'er like Carter as a running mate. If McGovern opted for the Southern running mate strategy (Kennedy and Johnson, for example), and was willing to let bygones be bygones, Carter as a moderate would certainly have been a possible choice. Carter was aware of this, and he did make a try to get on the ticket with McGovern. As he tells the story:

"At the time he [McGovern] was in the process of choosing a Vice-President, I called [Rep.] Andy Young [of Atlanta, a Carter supporter] asked Andy Young to help me put my name forward as a possible Vice-President.

"When my name was presented to McGovern, there was some vile language used and my name was immediately rejected, which was reported to me. I never tried anymore to have my name put forward."[5] (Julian Bond, who was one of the delegates at the convention, claimed that Carter told him twice in 1972 that he "wouldn't mind having his name mentioned" as a possible vice-presidential nominee on McGovern's ticket. However, Jody Powell, Carter's press secretary, denied that any such request was made to Bond.) Carter aides, Hamilton Jordan, Jerry Rafshoon, and Peter Bourne, also tried to get through to the McGovern camp. They went to the Doral Hotel where the presidential nominee was staying and managed to get a very brief appointment with McGovern's pollster, Patrick Caddell. At this time they showed him a somewhat dubious poll indicating that Carter would be McGovern's strongest running mate.[6] McGovern chose the ill-fated Eagleton, and the rest is history. McGovern went on to another damaging defeat for the Democrats, and Carter returned to Georgia to serve out the remainder of his term as governor and to begin preparations for Election '76.

Unless he tried for the presidency, Carter's political options were rather limited: by Georgia law he could not succeed himself as governor, and he had little hope of winning Herman Talmadge's seat in the U.S. Senate. So why not make a shot at the top office? In his autobiography he writes,

> I have always looked on the Presidency of the United States with reverence and awe, and I still do. But recently I have begun to realize that the president is just a human being. I can almost remember when I began to change my mind and form this opinion.
>
> Before becoming governor I had never met a president, although I once saw Harry Truman at a distance. . . . Then during 1971 and 1972 I met Richard Nixon, Spiro Agnew, George McGovern, Henry Jackson, Hubert Humphrey, Ed Muskie, George Wallace, Ronald Reagan, Nelson Rockefeller, and other presidential hopefuls, and I lost my feeling of awe about presidents. This is not meant as a criticism of them, but it is merely a simple statement of fact.[7]

Carter decided that he was just as qualified as the other candidates, and that perhaps the time had come when a Southerner could again be elected president. (The last president to hail from the Deep South had been Zachary Taylor in the 1850s.) George Wallace had demonstrated in 1968 and again in 1972 that a Southerner could be a strong contender in presidential politics. He had given voice to a mood of discontent and desire for change on the part of many, but his racist taint put him outside the mainstream of the Democratic party. Wallace had tapped the vein of a deep popular distrust of national leadership, which would grow in the next four years. However, he was not the man to lead the country in a more positive direction. Perhaps Carter was.

Back in Georgia Carter met with his wife and a small group of advisers to discuss his strengths and weaknesses, and he began working on a game plan to win the nomination of 1976. The plan emerged in a 70-page memorandum written largely by Hamilton Jordan, then Carter's executive secretary. It called for Carter to begin a course of study appropriate to a man with presidential aspirations. This included reading the major newspapers (*The New York Times, The Washington Post,* and *The Wall Street Journal*) every day, as well as books on such subjects as foreign affairs, defense, and economics. Carter also studied U.S. history and the presidency; with his usual thoroughness, he examined the campaign platforms of all the unsuccessful candidates for president since the beginning of the electoral process. He was to bone up on foreign policy under an adviser, and to meet foreign leaders on trade missions to Japan, Israel, South America, and Europe. A list of issues was drawn up, and task forces were assembled to prepare briefings on every issue, beginning in the *A*'s with abortion and continuing to the end of the alphabet.

Then there was the question of image. Carter was not well known nationally, but again, as in the 1970 gubernatorial race, this gave him flexibility in creating his own image. In 1973 he was to be "projected as the heaviest of the governors in accomplishments"; in 1974 "as a leader in the Democratic Party and someone involved in bringing it back"; in 1975 as a "heavyweight thinker, leader in the party who had some ideas for running the country"; and finally in 1976 as a presidential candidate.[8]

The nature of the opposition that Carter would face was also a topic of discussion, but here, "There was never any hesitancy about our plans because of other prospective candidates."[9] Senator Edward Kennedy was viewed as

Carter's strongest potential rival in the liberal camp. Thus on the very day he announced his candidacy, Carter had a talk with Kennedy about the Senator's plans for '76. At this time Kennedy told him that he had no intention of running. As for Senator Henry Jackson, whose views on a number of issues were similar to Carter's, Carter was advised to discontinue his practice of praising the senator in public, and to "be cautious to do nothing that might encourage him to run and make it plain that you have plans yourself."[10] Then there was Wallace. Carter's advisers hoped rather wistfully that perhaps Carter could get the Alabama governor's support if he saw Carter's candidacy as a sort of continuation of his own. But if Wallace decided to run again, he would be a major obstacle in Carter's path to the nomination.

While these plans were being laid, Carter also met with a man whose ideas on what constituted a successful campaign were very similar to his own. He was Joe Biden of Delaware, who had come out of nowhere to win a seat in the U.S. Senate in 1972, largely by telling voters they could trust him. Shortly after his election to the Senate, Biden spent several days with Carter at the governor's mansion in Atlanta, and the two men must have had some fairly interesting discussions about politics. Biden, who became chairman of Carter's national steering committee, says that as early as 1973 Carter was thinking in terms of a campaign based on sincerity and trust rather than discussion of specific issues. According to him, "Carter realized that it wasn't as important whether you were for or against busing, or abortion, or any issue as whether or not you demonstrated that you were bright and were someone people could trust."[11]

As we have seen, Carter had already been thinking along these lines in 1972 when he gave the nominating speech for Jackson. Joe Biden's campaign was for Carter simply a more recent example of the success of the "trust" approach that Kennedy had used in 1960. As the Watergate scandal unfolded, Carter would become even more convinced of the appropriateness of this type of campaign.

Carter was an outspoken critic of Nixon before the Watergate scandal. He called Nixon the poorest president to serve in his lifetime; blasted Nixon's revenue-sharing plan, describing it as a "cruel hoax" designed to conceal overall cutbacks in federal aid to the states; and attacked White House aide John Ehrlichman when he ignored Carter's request for an appointment to discuss the issue. Then on the morning of October 21, 1973, immediately after Nixon had fired Special Prosecuter Archibald Cox, Carter called a news conference and said that the firing of Cox was an action that warranted impeachment. He later went on national media to say that he thought Nixon was guilty and should resign.

But Carter had to do more than attack Nixon; he had to establish himself as a leader in his own right. At the National Governors Conference he attended while in office, Carter demonstrated his leadership abilities. His predecessor, Lester Maddox, had attracted attention at these conferences by doing such things as riding a bicycle backwards or announcing that he wouldn't attend a speech of Spiro Agnew's. This, however, was not Carter's way. He came to the fore by studying an emerging issue and becoming an expert on it before anyone else. Thus at the conference in 1971 he offered a resolution opposing making an issue of the war in Vietnam in the upcoming election. At another conference both he and Wallace offered antibusing resolutions. Most governors tended to look on the conferences as social occasions and didn't bother to bring their briefcases. Not Carter; he always came with a briefcase bulging with papers on a particular subject he had been boning up on.

However, Carter's capable performance at the National Governors Conference had little effect on his standing within the Democratic party. The game plan for 1974 called for his emergence as "a leader in the Democratic party and someone involved in bringing it back." With this in mind, Carter volunteered his services to National Committee Chairman Robert Strauss. Strauss was engaged in an effort to reestablish the broad base of the Democratic party, which had been shattered with McGovern's disastrous defeat. Strauss had already hired North Carolina Governor Terry Sanford (who had run as a "Stop Wallace" presidential candidate in 1972) to help with preparations for the 1974 congressional and gubernatorial elections. But he readily accepted Carter's offer of aid. Carter and Sanford were the "names" on the 1974 Campaign Committee's letterhead; the staff consisted of Carter's assistant, Hamilton Jordan, and Robert Keefe, who was on loan from the National Committee. (Keefe later went on to become Henry Jackson's campaign manager in 1976.)

Of his work as chairman of the Campaign Committee, Carter writes in his autobiography,

> During 1973 and 1974 I met frequently with leaders of groups who ordinarily support Democratic candi-

dates. These leaders, from about twenty-five different organizations, represented labor unions, farmers, Spanish-Americans, teachers, environmentalists, women, local officials, retired persons, government workers, blacks and the House and Senate campaign committees.

Four or five of the major opinion pollsters worked closely with me, and helped to delineate the most important issues among the American electorate as the elections approached. With the help of a volunteer staff, we recruited several experts in each of about thirty issue subjects to give me their opinions of what our nation should do about that particular question, and then we edited those disparate suggestions into one coherent issue paper on each subject.[12]

At meetings with leaders of the various groups supporting Democratic candidates, Carter was very effective because he was low-keyed, friendly, and knowledgeable without being opinionated. In contrast, Sanford was not effective on a one-to-one basis because of a tendency to talk down to people. Carter wrote personal notes to the various leaders he met as a follow-up, and thus he initiated a communication process. Sanford did not. Carter paid all his expenses, while Sanford was paid by the Democratic National Committee.

When campaign time came, Carter worked personally with over 60 of the campaigns, making speeches for the different candidates. His speeches were clearly aimed at pushing the particular candidate and the Democratic party rather than advancing himself. He did not undercut other people or possible candidates, but instead worked as an organization builder. He made important friendships that would be helpful to him later, though at the same time no one thought of him as a presidential candidate. Also, by listening and talking to people, he obtained excellent firsthand knowledge of the various states and their problems. He writes, "All of this was . . . a good learning experience for me." There is no doubt that it was.

While he was making new contacts within the party, Carter made a point of breaking off an old one. At the last National Governors Conference he attended while in office, he presented a list of reasons as to why Wallace could not win either the Democratic presidential nomination or the vice-presidential nomination. The Alabama governor had made a good showing in the '72 presidential primaries. In the '76 race his health would be a definite drawback, but he still had a following strong enough to inspire fear in the hearts of the other prospective candidates. Carter knew he would have to beat Wallace in order to win himself. As early as June, 1974, at the National Governors Conference in Seattle (which Wallace, by the way, did not attend) he began to draw the lines of battle between them. The Wallace connection had served him well in the past, but the time had come to sever it and to emerge as the antiestablishment candidate.

In November, 1974, many of the Democratic candidates, on whose campaigns Carter had worked, were elected to office. Their victories were a clear demonstration of the success of the "Trust me" approach, which Carter had advocated. Having made his contribution, Carter was now ready to move on his own behalf. A month later on December 12, 1974, in a speech entitled, "For

America's Third Century Why Not the Best?" Carter
formally announced his candidacy.

In this speech he sounded the discontent that many felt
with government in the wake of Vietnam and the Watergate disclosures:

> Recently we have discovered that our trust has been
> betrayed. The veils of secrecy have seemed to thicken
> around Washington. The purposes and the goals of our
> country are uncertain and sometimes even suspect.
>
> Our people are understandably concerned with this
> lack of competence and integrity. The root of the prob-
> lem is not so much that our people have lost confidence
> in government, but that government has demonstrated
> time and again its lack of confidence in the people.
>
> Our political leaders have simply underestimated the
> innate quality of our people.
>
> With the shame of Watergate still with us and our
> 200th birthday just ahead, it is time for us to reaffirm
> and to strengthen our ethical and spiritual and political
> beliefs.
>
> There must be no lowering of these standards, no
> acceptance of mediocrity in any aspect of our private or
> public lives.
>
> In our homes or at worship we are ever reminded of
> what we ought to do and what we ought to be. Our
> government can and must represent the best and the
> highest ideals of those of us who voluntarily submit to
> its authority.
>
> Politicians who seek to further their political careers
> through appeals to our doubts, fears, and prejudices
> will be exposed and rejected.
>
> For too long political leaders have been isolated from
> the people. They have made decisions from an ivory

tower. Few have ever seen personally the direct impact of government programs involving welfare, prisons, mental institutions, unemployment, school busing, or public housing. Our people feel that they have little access to the core of government and little influence with elected officials.

Now is the time for this chasm between people and government to be bridged, and for American citizens to join in shaping our nation's future.

Now is the time for new leadership and new ideas to make a reality of these dreams, still held by our people.

To begin with, the confidence of people in our own government must be restored. But too many officials do not deserve that confidence.

There is a simple and effective way for public officials to regain public trust — be trustworthy!

Carter's speech was at once right for the times and completely in character. The Populist tradition, from which he stemmed, had called for a government that was more responsive to the ordinary citizen, so often neglected. Yet while Wallace and other Southern Populists before him had appealed to people's darker instincts — to their fears and prejudices — Carter invoked all that was best in human nature. Comparing twentieth-century Americans with their eighteenth-century forebears, he raised the question:

Were they more competent, more intelligent, or better educated than we? Were they more courageous? Did they have more compassion or love for their neighbors? Did they have deeper religious convictions? Were they more concerned about the future of their children than we?

I think not.

We are equally capable of correcting our faults, overcoming difficulties, managing our own affairs, and facing the future with justifiable confidence.

I am convinced that among us 200 million Americans there is a willingness — even eagerness — to restore in our country what has been lost — *if* we have understandable purposes and goals and a modicum of bold and inspired leadership.

Our government can express the highest common ideals of human beings — *if* we demand of it standards of excellence. . . ..

For our Nation — for all of us — the question is, Why not the best?

In his announcement speech Carter successfully combined the populism of George Wallace with the call for excellence of a Kennedy. The times they were a'changing, and Jimmy Carter spoke for that change. He was indeed a "new voice from the South."

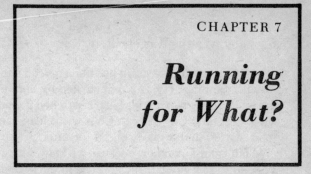

CHAPTER 7

Running for What?

When the word got out that Jimmy Carter was going to take a shot at the presidency, it gave an old foe of Carter's from the 1970 campaign an opportunity at a different kind of shot. *Atlanta Constitution* editor Reg Murphy wrote a column entitled, "Jimmy Carter's Running for What?" It began like this: "Governor Jimmy Carter's timing was just right. The state needed a good bellylaugh, and Carter obliged by announcing he would run for president."[1]

Georgia governors tend to go in on a wave and out on a rail, and Jimmy Carter was no exception. He had made his share of enemies during his term as governor. There were those who didn't think he could get elected dogcatcher, let alone president. But he had his friends, too. When Carter announced his candidacy, Jack Spalding, editor of the *Atlanta Journal*, wrote, "I do not see anything peculiar in Jimmy Carter trying for the presidential nomination though a lot of people I talk to seem to think it's funny. But they're not faced with the prospect of returning to the farm unless something better turns up." In a more serious vein, Spalding continued,

> The land hungers for leadership and like his methods or not, Gov. Carter always has known where he wanted

to go and what he was about.
. . . .

The Carter administration has been a good one, critics notwithstanding. It has been marked by high purpose and while the performance hasn't matched the purpose, the governor is going to come out with clean hands and good marks, and a great big E for effort.

We fault our governor because we know him well and we tend to place our trust in those like Richard Nixon whose television image is all we know. You'd think we'd learn.[2]

Still the question remained: How does an unemployed governor, not particularly popular in his own state, go about launching a presidential campaign? The answer, according to the game plan devised in 1972, was for Jimmy to take to the road, adopting a "learning posture . . . you don't pretend to . . . know everything and that a major aspect of your campaign will be to travel the country . . . and learn."[3] Carter's lack of employment actually worked to his advantage because as of January, 1975, he was able to campaign full time. The schedule for '75 called for 250 days of campaigning with visits to 40 states and 200 cities and towns. The year before, in his work for the 1974 Democratic National Campaign Committee, Carter had traveled the country and made some friends that he could look up this time around. The groundwork had already been laid, though no one knew it at that time. Carter describes the '75 effort thus:

Our strategy was simple: make a total effort all over the nation. After leaving office as governor, during the first months alone, I visited more than half the states,

some of them several times. Each visit was carefully
planned — by my small Atlanta staff and a local volunteer in each community — to be included during the
week's trip. Our purposes during this early stage of the
campaign were: to become known among those who
have a continuing interest in politics and government;
to recruit supporters and to raise campaign funds; and
to obtain maximum news coverage for myself and my
stand on the many local and national issues. The most
important purpose of all was for me to learn this
nation — what it is, and what it ought to be.[4]

During these trips Carter made a good impression on
voters, who responded to his apparent warmth and sincerity, but weren't always sure where he stood on specific
issues. In his efforts to make himself better known and to
establish a positive image, Carter was actually aided by
the other candidates, notably Henry Jackson. He saw
Carter as a "stalking horse" who would hold Jackson
supporters in line until the following spring when the
senator would launch an active campaign of his own, and
easily eliminate Carter. Thus in at least three states —
New Hampshire, Florida, and Pennsylvania — Jackson
supporters temporarily aided the Carter campaign. The
case of Florida is particularly interesting. Here Carter
was able to persuade the other candidates not to campaign actively in the state for several months, and thus
leave the field open for a one-to-one duel between himself
and Wallace. By eliminating Wallace, Carter would be
helping out the other candidates who feared the Alabama
governor, but did not similarly fear Carter. By the time
they realized their mistake, it would be too late.

Most of the money that financed Carter's first year of campaigning came from fellow Georgians who, then as later on, provided the mainstay of his finances. Contributions were modest in the beginning with few over $1,000. (Among those who did contribute $1,000 or more were Charles Kirbo, Carter's long-time political mentor; Hamilton Jordan, his campaign manager; and Robert Lipschutz, a wealthy Atlanta attorney who became campaign treasurer.) Nevertheless, by January, 1976, Carter had raised the necessary $5,000 in states through contributions of $250 or less which made him eligible for his first federal matching funds. Since Carter could not expect any "big money" in the beginning, the Federal Matching Funds were crucial to the financing of his campaign. Without them it would have been extremely difficult for him to make the nationwide effort that he did.

While he was charming voters across the country with his smile, Carter was also at work, building from his grass-roots campaign a formidable political organization. This accomplishment would later prompt columnist James Reston to call him "Mayor Daley in the binding of a hymn book." Organization was an important step because under the new system of proliferating primaries, a candidate had to have a good political organization in each state in which he wanted to win delegates. George Wallace had suffered in 1972 in spite of his strong popular support because he lacked effective state and local organization, and thus arrived at the Democratic convention without much backing.

The success of Carter's early-start campaign was evident by the time of the National Democratic Issues Conference in November, 1975. At this time Robert Walters observed in an article in *National Journal:* "When jockeying for the nomination began early in this year, Carter was regarded widely as a weak and frivolous candidate who was not to be taken seriously by either his fellow contenders or the voters. In recent months, however, he has emerged as a strong and serious campaigner who is now ranked as one of the approximately half-dozen men currently leading the race for the nomination."[5]

At the Issues Conference, Carter impressed audiences as being more articulate and better informed on the issues than many of the old pro's. In a panel discussion, for instance, with Senator Henry Jackson and former ambassador Sargent Shriver, Carter more than held his own. He had done his homework well since he had begun his presidential prep course back in 1972.

Three months later Carter's campaign was off to a good start when he came out ahead in the Iowa caucuses held on January 19. In Mississippi, however, he came in second, well behind Wallace. The primaries loomed ahead.

Unlike the other candidates, Carter and his strategists believed that there would not be a brokered convention in '76. Instead the party's nominee would emerge from the long, arduous process of primaries and state caucuses. Therefore, they adopted a high-risk strategy of running everywhere, hoping to pick up enough delegate support to insure Carter's nomination at Madison Square Garden in July. By running everywhere Carter risked spreading himself too thin. On the other hand, since he would be in the race every Tuesday he had a chance to exchange one week's defeat for another week's victory. Also, if he did well in the early primaries, his campaign would build important momentum. Once he got rolling and showed himself to be a winner, there were many who would be ready to jump on the Carter bandwagon.

The rest of Carter's strategy was based on two things: first, his determination to avoid the mistakes of past Democratic presidential candidates, notably McGovern; second, his reading of the current national mood. The system of proliferating primaries, instituted in the wake of the holocaust at the 1968 Democratic Convention in Chicago, had made possible the emergence of a dark-horse candidate like McGovern. Yet through his political extremism, McGovern had alienated important elements within the party and within the electorate at large. Carter had no intention of repeating McGovern's errors; instead he decided to follow a middle-of-the-road path like Kennedy. This course included slight deviations to the right and the left when it would help him. His economic policies were moderate to conservative, and he was conservative on such things as abortion and the death penalty. Yet he took liberal stances as far as withdrawing U.S. troops from Korea and decriminalizing marijuana. Taken as a whole, Carter's positions on the issues were designed to appeal to the greatest number of voters possible. Interestingly enough, the liberal candidates in the race — Morris Udall, Birch Bayh, Sargent Shriver, and Fred Harris — claimed to have learned the lesson of '72 also. They would avoid extreme positions, they said; yet their economic policies were much more radical than any put forward by McGovern in 1972. Even Senator Henry Jackson, a more or less moderate candidate (more conservative than the liberals on social issues but tougher on defense and foreign policy), advanced economic policies that, like those of the liberals, involved heavy government spending.

As Carter's rival for the moderate to conservative vote, Jackson could point to 30 years of experience in Washington. Carter, on the other hand, picked up on the anti-Washington sentiment in the country, and stressed his lack of Washington credentials and the fact that he wasn't a lawyer. However, he was careful not to go too far in his criticism of Washington because he knew he would need the support of the Georgetown set later on.

To voters disillusioned by Vietnam and Watergate, Carter presented himself as a man of integrity, someone whom they could trust. "I'll never tell a lie," he told audiences, "I'll never betray your trust. I'll never make a misleading statement or avoid a controversial issue." It was a daring statement to make because it meant that Carter would receive greater scrutiny than the other candidates. Everything he said or didn't say would be weighed against the high standard of openness and honesty, which he himself had set. Still, Carter took the chance because he believed that the voters were more concerned with a candidate's character than they were with his stands on specific issues.

In addition to trust, Carter spoke of love and goodness. A typical campaign speech ended on this note: "I don't want anything selfish out of government. I think I want the same thing you do. And that is to have our nation once again with a government as good and honest and decent and truthful and fair and competent and idealistic and compassionate, and as filled with love, as are the American people." McGovern had spoken of love, too, but as Catholic theologian Michael Novak pointed out, Carter's style was much "less threatening" than McGovern's: He [Carter] does not seek to 'purify,' but to 'heal' and bring 'love.' When McGovern spoke of 'love,' it had a punitive, reforming ring. Carter's tone offers warmth and consolation."[6]

Carter's talk of love and trust drew an astonished reaction from the columnists. "I have never seen a candidate like him," anounced *Christian Science Monitor* columnist TRB. "Love is Sweeping the Country," wrote David Broder of the *Washington Post*, observing that Jimmy Carter was the first presidential candidate since William Wintergreen, hero of the 1930s musical *Of Thee I Sing*, to talk about bringing love to the White House. Yet Broder saw the wolf beneath the sheep's clothing; behind the mawkish talk of love and trust there lurked — in Broder's words — "a throughly tough, opportunist politician, who comes into almost any competition with his elbows out." Broder also recognized the "genius" of Carter's insight "that, after the spiritual travails of the past decade, voters are ready to listen to someone who can talk, without visible embarassment, of something as simple and basic as love."[7]

The fact was that Carter's unique appeal was having its effect. TRB observed audiences "yearning" to believe. Political writer, Richard Reeves, wrote that the yearning crowds included "a surprisingly high proportion of the working press. We want to believe, too."[8]

Still, was it enough to warm voter's hearts in the small, snowbound state of New Hampshire, where the first primary would be held? As primary day approached, 100 supporters came up from Georgia to tromp through the snow, distributing bags of peanuts and pushing their candidate. Also braving the freezing temperatures was Carter's old enemy, Lester Maddox, there to expose Carter as a concealed "radical liberal." "He's two-faced, he's the biggest phony I've ever known, and I just hope to God the American people find out before it's too late."

In New Hampshire the liberal vote (59%) was split four ways between Udall, Bayh, Shriver, and Harris; while Carter had the moderate to conservative territory (41% of the vote) pretty much to himself. Carter's friendly, low-keyed campaigning style also stood him in good stead in this small state. As one voter commented: "His [Carter's] essence is that he is perceived as a conservative — old fashioned values, family, patriotism, religion — and has also engaged some liberals. . . ."[9] In fact, Carter's base of support was broad. He ran strong among several groups — blue collar workers, older people, those with a grade-school education, and those who favored a balanced federal budget. Carter rather than another liberal was the second choice of many Bayh supporters. In industrial Manchester, Carter came out ahead of Bayh and Udall with 3,239 votes compared to Bayh's 2,567, and Udall's 1,843. When the final tally came in, Carter had won a plurality of the vote (30%), with 24% going to Udall, 16% to Bayh, 11% to Harris, and 9% to Shriver.[10]

The next big test for the peanut farmer-turned-politician came in the Florida primary on March 9. Here the picture did not look promising. A pre-primary poll showed Wallace getting 35% of the vote to Carter's 30%. Jackson was also in the running, but he had entered the contest too late to have much impact. He also had the image of a loser to Wallace from the 1972 campaign in the state. Victory over Wallace was crucial to Carter's chances of getting the nomination. He had to defeat Wallace in Florida, a state that was important as one of the newly populous and politically potent sunbelt states; otherwise, he would face serious challenges from the Alabama governor in other Southern states as well as states like Michigan and Indiana, where Wallace had done well in 1972. Fortunately for Carter, he wasn't the only one who wanted to see Wallace lose. Liberal California multimillionaire Max Pavelsky, who backed McGovern in '72, helped finance an early and effective advertising campaign in Florida. Liberal labor unions and some of the black political leaders also supported Carter on a short-term basis in his anti-Wallace drive. Notable among the black leaders were Representative Andrew Young of Georgia, who decided to continue his support after Florida; and Georgia State Senator Julian Bond, who afterwards shifted his endorsement to Morris Udall.

In the Florida campaign, Carter was careful not to attack the Wallace "message"; rather he stressed the fact that he, instead of the Alabama governor, had a real chance to be elected president. He did not want to alienate Wallace supporters; he also wanted to make it possible for Wallace to support him later on. Again, as in New Hampshire, Carter was perceived as a moderate to conservative candidate. He had the black vote (blacks represented 15.3% of the population) pretty much to himself because blacks were alienated by Jackson's stong antibusing stance. In addition to winning 72% of the black vote, Carter attracted the majority of young voters, blue collar workers, and those who had incomes of less than $15,000. He also did well among Democrats who had moved to

Florida from other parts of the South, and he ran even with Wallace among people born in Florida. No one issue proved decisive in Carter's victory except that his backers were more sympathetic than all Florida Democrats to federal aid to blacks. (In a book called *The Ethnic Factor: How America's Minorities Decide Elections*, M. R. Levy and Michael S. Kramer show that in the 1972 senatorial race the black vote won the election in Florida for Lawton Childs against a better-known, well-financed campaigner, William C. Kramer, when the issue was support for the 1964 Civil Rights Act.) Contrary to what the polls had originally predicted, Carter won 34% of the vote, Wallace 31%, and Jackson 24%.[11]

A week later in Illinois, Carter scored another upset victory over Wallace. Polls taken a week before the primary had showed the Alabama governor ahead with Carter gaining. Wallace's paralysis was a factor, as 4 out of 10 Democrats said they were worried about the Alabama governor's health. Carter's greatest strength was in Northwestern Illinois, a prosperous farming area with politically moderate cities like Rockford, Moline, and Galesburg. Here his own farm background obviously helped. Nevertheless, Carter more than held his own in Cook County (Chicago and its suburbs), even though Mayor Daley was running a favorite-son slate with Adlai Stevenson, Jr. Carter also ran strongly among blacks, who represented more than half of the Democratic vote in Illinois. He polled one-half of the black vote, which was twice as much as Shriver, who had good credentials among blacks because of his work in the federal antipoverty program. All in all, Carter won 48% of the vote, Wallace 28%, and Shriver 16%.[12]

George Wallace had shrunk a little since 1968 and 1972, but he was still enough of a political Goliath to give the man who could beat him a reputation as a giant killer. With his victories in Florida, Illinois, and later in North Carolina, Carter proved that he was such a giant killer, but the truth was that many liberals were unhappy with their David. Even before Carter's victory in New Hampshire, a series of articles that were highly critical of him had begun to appear. Typical of the attack on Carter was Steven Brill's "Jimmy Carter's Pathetic Lies," a piece which appeared in the March issue of *Harper's*. In this article Brill exposed the "dirty tricks" Carter had used against Sanders in the 1970 gubernatorial campaign, picked apart Carter's record as governor, and in general portrayed him as a man who believed in nothing but himself: "Jimmy Carter's campaign — hungry, no philosophy, and brilliantly packaged — *is* Jimmy Carter."[13]

In any presidential campaign a candidate could expect a certain amount of adverse comment, but in the '76 race, the liberal assault on Jimmy Carter was, according to *Washington Star* political writer Jack Germond, "perhaps unmatched in harshness and intensity in any presidential campaign of the postwar period."[14]

Some of the charges against Carter were, in fact, legitimate. He did have a tendency to exaggerate his accomplishments. He described himself as a *nuclear physicist* when *nuclear engineer* would have been the more appropriate term since he hadn't received a Ph.D. He said he had cut down the number of government agencies from 300 to 22, when in reality there had only been 65 budgeted agencies when he started out.

He also showed himself to be a bit of a trimmer. Thus when he spoke to black audiences, Carter was sure to include Martin Luther King, Jr.'s, name in his list of great Americans; but when he addressed all-white audiences in the South, King's name mysteriously disappeared. In addition, Carter was capable of subtle rhetorical shadings, designed to make his positions acceptable to the greatest number of people. In his position on amnesty, for example, he made a distinction between amnesty and pardon, where according to the dictionary no such distinction existed. Carter said he would grant a pardon to all draft resistors instead of amnesty because "Amnesty says what you did was right. Pardon says whether what you did was right or wrong you are forgiven for it." Carter understood that the time had come for the country to put Vietnam behind it; but he still did not want to alienate, as George McGovern had done, all those whose sons had served in Vietnam, regardless of whether or not they thought the war was right.

There was also the whole question of Carter's stand on the Vietnam War, which represented an obvious shift from the past. During the 1976 campaign, Carter was fond of saying, "The American people did not make a decision to go into the war in Vietnam and Cambodia and spend 50,000 American lives and 150 billion dollars, but it happened." He also called the war "racist," explaining that because the skins of the Vietnamese were yellow, it was easier for U.S. troops to kill them than it would have been if they had been white. Yet while the war was going on, Carter was definitely not one of its outspoken critics. As late as 1974, he was still telling journalists that he favored more military appropriations for the war effort.

However, Carter wasn't the only Democratic candidate to have been "wrong" on an issue in the past. Nor was he the only one to exaggerate his record or do a bit of trimming here and there. Why then did the liberals single him out for attack? Jack Germond attempted to explain: "The answer may be that he is such a different political animal. He cannot be categorized on issues in any comfortable way. He is a liberal on health insurance and the environment and gun control, and he has Andrew Young on his side. But he is 'conservative' on abortion and amnesty and shaky on the death penalty."[15]

But Carter's stands on the issues weren't the only reason the liberals didn't like him: "Carter is alien, too, because he comes on so strong, so implacably self-assured and apparently independent of the system. To conventional politicians he is a threatening outsider, and they are clearly outraged at his attempts to pass himself off as just folks from Plains, Ga., when they have discovered he knows many of their best tricks."[16]

Germond went on to explain that "In the plays of Tennessee Williams the protagonist is often an outsider, a foreign presence, sometimes a Sicilian. And the fact that he brings a different ethic to the community sets in motion all the traumatic dislocations of personal and social relationships that make the drama." For Germond, "In the campaign of 1976, Jimmy Carter is a political Sicilian."[17]

However, the liberals weren't the only ones who didn't like Carter. The Washington establishment didn't like him because, according to Charles Morgan, head of the Washington office of the American Civil Liberties Union, they didn't have their hooks into him. Labor didn't like him because of his stand on right-to-work laws; and there was no love lost between Carter and several of his fellow governors. Reubin Askew was cool towards Carter because Carter had once tried to block Askew's election as head of the Southern Governors' Conference. Maryland Governor Marvin Mandel also disliked Carter because Carter had tried to get in the way of his election as head of the Governors' Conference. (Carter had supported Dolph Briscoe of Texas instead, and this turned out to be important for him in the '76 campaign when Briscoe supported him in the Texas primary.) Mandel was to launch a vigorous "Stop Carter" campaign that reached its climax with the entry of California Governor Jerry Brown into the Maryland primary.

Who then did like Jimmy Carter? The answer was some — but not all of the Southern liberals and blacks. How a Southerner like Carter could attract the strong support of blacks as he did was a problem that perplexed many a Northern liberal. Black support for Carter in the Florida primary could be explained away as an anti-Wallace vote. However, in other primaries Carter polled a large percentage of the black vote — 47.6 percent in Illinois and 41.5 percent in Massachusetts. Certain things obviously helped Carter with blacks: his excellent record in the area of race relations while governor; the fact that he had the endorsement of Congressman Andrew Young and Martin Luther King, Sr.; and also that he had about a dozen blacks, some of them in high positions, on his campaign staff.

Nevertheless, aside from Andrew Young, Carter did not have the support of major black political leaders. He managed to bypass the leaders and appeal directly to the people. Alone among the candidates, Carter consistently went to black churches and actually preached to them; and this, as black columnist William Raspberry pointed out, meant more than Mo Udall appearing with Shirley Chisholm.[18] In the churches, Carter's Southern Baptist Evangelist style struck a chord within God-fearing working-class blacks. "Jimmy Carter has got soul," commented the Reverend T. Garret Benjamin after Carter had addressed a black audience at the Second Christian Church in Indianapolis. In some cases Carter didn't have to go directly to a church himself to win the support of its congregation. *Washington Post* writer Richard Cohen gives the example of the Plymouth Congregational Church in the Washington, D.C., area.[19] Here Carter campaign literature was passed out with the implicit "blessing of the pastor," the Reverend Theodore S. Ledbetter. In addition to Ledbetter, about 50 other ministers in the area were appealed to — some by Carter workers, but others by friends and colleagues. The blessings of many pastors in black communities provided an important source of support for Carter.

Carter depended heavily upon his black support to reach other elements within the Democratic party that were either unsure or openly hostile toward him: elected officials, white Northern liberals, and labor union leaders. Sensing a winner, individuals from these different groups in the party began to join the Carter camp after his victories over Wallace and liberal candidates Birch Bayh, Fred Harris, and Sargent Shriver. Theodore Sorenson, a Northern liberal long associated with the Kennedys, joined up. Leonard Woodcock, president of the United Auto Workers, appeared favorably disposed towards Carter; and Carter was even able to open up a dialogue with AFL-CIO President George Meany, who had earlier refused to speak to him. Others appeared to be gravitating toward Carter. The record of campaign contributions for the month of March showed increasing support from the financial and Democratic establishments in New York and California. By the end of March, Carter was riding high. Then came April and the furor over *ethnic purity*.

The ill-chosen phrase first appeared in an interview published in the *New York Daily News*. In response to a question about low-income, scatter-site housing in the suburbs, Carter said, "I see nothing wrong with ethnic purity being maintained. I would not force a racial integration of a neighborhood by government action. But I would not permit discrimination against a family moving into a neighborhood."[20] There was nothing "wrong" with Carter's position here, but the phrase *ethnic purity* seemed to have racist and even Hitlerian connotations. It was picked up by a CBS official, and the network's correspondent, Ed Rabel, proceeded to grill Carter as to exactly what he meant by *ethnic purity*. The flak that resulted looked as if it might have serious effects on Carter's campaign. The candidate's main black supporter, Andrew Young, called the phrase a "disaster"; and the Black Congressional Caucus and such prominent black leaders as Vernon Jordan of the National Urban League protested vigorously. White Northern liberals who had suspected Carter of being a "scrubbed-over" Wallace all along produced a chorus of "I-told-you-so's."

However, Carter handled the situation well. He apologized immediately for the phrase, and his black supporters seemed ready to forget and forgive. At a rally in Atlanta, Carter and Martin Luther King, Sr., joined in a soul handshake. Said the father of the slain civil rights leader, "I have a forgiving heart, so I'm with you all the way." The uproar over *ethnic purity* subsided, and in the final analysis the remark did not appear to hurt Carter in the way that George Romney's "brainwash" statement in the 1968 campaign or McGovern's "1,000 percent" remark in 1972 harmed their respective candidacies. In spite of *ethnic purity* Carter won a majority of the black vote in the District of Columbia primary later on, which was generally regarded as a popularity contest between black Mayor Walter Washington and Congressman Walter Fauntroy. Apparently the roots of Carter's black support went deep enough so as not to be seriously disturbed by one remark.

As for the two primaries in that first week of April, Carter lost New York to Jackson, but won a narrow victory over Udall in Wisconsin — so narrow in fact that Udall was prematurely declared the winner. In New York Jackson was the favorite of the moderates and conservatives (one-half of the vote) and Udall of the liberals; Carter drew support from all three groups. The decisive Jewish vote (40% of the total) went almost entirely to Jackson (70%).[21]

A poll that appeared in *Time* magazine on March 8 showed Udall winning in Wisconsin. According to the poll, Udall and Wallace were in a "dead heat" while the other candidates — Jackson, Carter, Bayh, and Harris — lagged far behind. Udall had been building up an organization months before the others, who only came in after the Florida primary. Udall also outspent the other candidates in terms of radio and TV advertising. He won two-thirds of the "elite" liberal vote, which consisted of college graduates and professionals. Carter was the favorite candidate of the moderates and conservatives; again he had a broad base of support. He beat Udall by only two percentage points.[22] Yet his victory was significant because it demonstrated that he could defeat the main liberal contender in one of the most progressive of all states.

The real contest, however, lay ahead in the Pennsylvania primary at the end of the month. At this point in the race, Carter had won 6 out of 8 primaries and rated high in the opinion polls, running neck and neck with Hubert Humphrey, who as yet had not entered a primary. Humphrey would be a formidable opponent because he was popular with the liberals, blacks, and labor. The time seemed ripe for a showdown between Carter and the Happy Warrior. Thus in Pennsylvania Carter faced a "stop" coalition consisting of the major labor unions and the state and local political bosses. This coalition backed Jackson, but with an ulterior motive. What they really hoped to do was bring Humphrey into the field.

In Pennsylvania the *Time* pre-primary poll of March 8 showed that no one was leading among the Democrats, but that the Jackson effort was well organized and well financed. Wallace remained a threat (this was before the Florida and Illinois primaries); the liberal vote was split between Bayh and Udall; Carter's local organization was amateurish. Well aware of the importance of a Pennsylvania victory, Carter campaigned hard in the state in the weeks prior to the primary. He attacked the political bosses, especially Philadelphia Mayor Frank Rizzo (who was unpopular with the majority of voters in the state, anyway). He launched an extensive television and radio advertising campaign, which gave him an edge over Jackson and Udall. All three candidates were hurt when Federal Matching Funds were cut off after a Supreme Court decision declared a portion of the law unconstitutional, and President Ford took his time in submitting new legislation. However, the Carter organization made careful plans to raise the necessary money to finance its advertising campaign through fund-raising efforts in Georgia and New York.

Carter's Pennsylvania effort proved remarkably successful: he polled 36% of the vote, Jackson 26%, Udall 19%, and Wallace 11%.[23] Carter carried 66 of the state's 67 counties, and again demonstrated his ability to appeal to a wide range of voters — to white collar and blue collar workers, to young and old, to Protestants and Roman Catholics. (Jackson did well with the Jews, but they represented a very small percentage of the vote.) Carter's Evangelist religion helped him with Protestant voters; he did especially well with those of German and Pennsylvania Dutch ancestry, many of whom were Fundamentalists. Carter's earlier victories over Wallace also helped him. In 1972 the Alabama governor had come in second with 21% of the vote; in 1976, however, he came in fourth with one-third of his supporters switching to Carter. Carter's *ethnic purity* remark did not hurt him with black voters in Pennsylvania. He won 40% of the black vote (blacks represented 8.6% of the population in the state, but 20.7% in Pittsburgh and 34.4% in Philadelphia), which was only a slight slip from the New York primary where he got one-half of the black vote.[24] Carter's cause with blacks was aided by the fact that several prominent black leaders came into the state to campaign for him. Although the union leaders backed Jackson, Carter got more than half of the union membership vote.

After Pennsylvania, Jackson decided to step out of the

Jimmy Carter campaigning in Florida

Magnum

Charles M. Ráfshoon

Above: The Carter family store in Plains, Georgia,
run by Earl Carter (1925); *below:* Interior of
the Carter store (1925)

Charles M. Rafs

Charles M. Rafshoon

Lillian and Earl Carter, Jimmy's parents

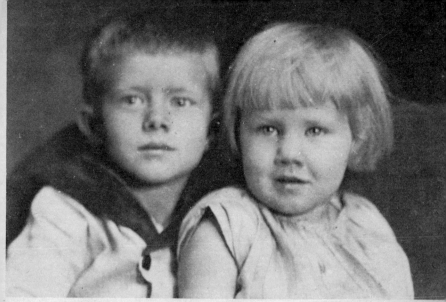

Above: Jimmy (age 5) with his sister Gloria (age 3); *right:* Jimmy Carter, one year old; *Opposite:* Lillian Carter holding Jimmy

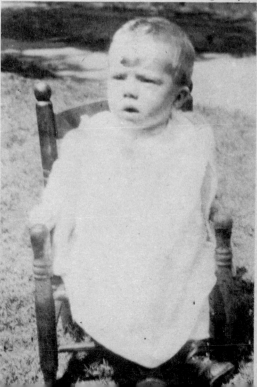

Columbus Ledger-Enquirer

Columbus Ledger-Enquirer

Columbus Ledger-Enq

Opposite, far left: Jimmy (at about age 9) riding Lady in the backyard of his home; *Opposite, right:* Jimmy, with his dog Bozo (1937); *Opposite, below:* Jimmy, with his brother Billy; *right:* Carter as a U.S. Naval midshipman; *below:* Jimmy Carter with the "O" Division aboard the USS *Wyoming* (June, 1947)

Columbus Ledger-Enquirer

Charles M. Rafshoon

Left: Rear Admiral Hyman
Rickover, a man who Carter
feels had a profound effect [
his life; *below:* Jimmy Carte
with members of his Subma[
School class (1948)

Wide World

Charles M. Rafsh[

Carter aboard a submarine at sea (1948)

Charles M. Rafsh

Charles M. Rafshoon

Above: Jimmy working at the Carter Warehouse in Plains (1968); *right:* Jimmy Carter, peanut farmer (1968)

Former Georgia Governor Carl Sanders being doused with champagne by black Atlanta Hawks basketball player. It is generally believed that the Carter campaign committee circulated this photo in an attempt to show that Sanders' sympathies were with blacks

Above: Carter announces that he will again be candidate for governor of Georgia (1970); *left:* Carter with early returns for gubernatorial primary; *below:* Former Georgia Governor Lester Maddox rides a bike backwards as he takes in the historic centers as a sightseer before the start of the 35th Annual Southern Governors Conference (1969)

bove, Jimmy and Rosalynn
arter greet supporters at
imary headquarters;
ght, Governor Carter backed
Georgia flag

Right: Carter on a trampoline with his daughter Amy (1974); *below:* Carter tossing a Frisbee with his son Jack (1974)

Columbus Ledger-Enquirer

Jimmy strolls through the woods with his wife and son Jeff

Right, Governor Carter with his choice, David Gambrell, for vacant Senate seat; *below*, Askew and Carter at National Governors' Conference, 1972

Wide World

Wide World

Right, Governors Wallace and Carter in Washington; *below*, Signing Georgia Senate resolution against forced busing

Magnum

Above, Former Governor Carter at New Hampshire primary headquarters.
Opposite: *above*, Campaigning for Jewish vote in Chicago; *below left*, Listening to
choir at Chicago church; *below right*, With Peter Rodino, chairman of the House
Judiciary Committee (1975)

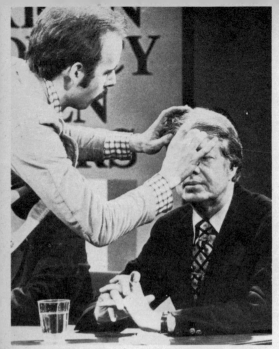

Left, A touchup before appearin
on television — Wisconsin
presidential primary; *below*, Th
two front-running presidential
hopefuls, Carter and Udall (Apr
1976). Opposite: *above*, Three
Democratic presidential
contenders: Carter between
liberal Udall and traditional
southerner Wallace; *below*,
Shaking hands with a worker a
the chevrolet plant in
Indianapolis

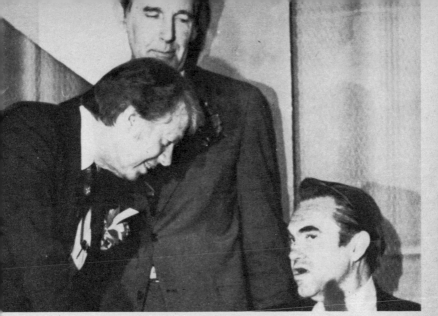

Above: Carter moving from one Ohio campaign location to another; *Opposite, above:*
Touring a factory in New Hampshire; *Opposite, below:* Comfortable politicking in
North Carolina

Opposite: Carter with New York City's Mayor Beame, after receiving Beame's endorsement (1976); *right:* With Hubert Humphrey of Minnesota at Democratic congressional dinner (1976); *below:* Carter listening to the views of some Georgia residents (1970)

Joe Heiberger, Washington Post

s M. Rafshoon

Charles M. Raf[

The Carters pose for a family portrait. *Seated, from left to right:* Rosalynn, Amy, Jimmy, Annette, and Jeff; *Standing:* Chip, Caron, Jason, Jack, and Judy

Carter receiving the enthusiastic approval of
Dr. Martin Luther King, Sr. (Atlanta, 1976)

Carter applauding rock star Gregg Allman after Allman's performance during
Carter's four-hour telethon. Allman was one of many celebrities to perform in the
telethon, which raised in excess of a quarter million dollars (1976)

Charles M. Rafshoon

Carter with his mother Lillian, wife Rosalynn, and daughter Amy at their home in Plains (1975)

Maxwell Silverstein

Two of the many political cartoons that have appeared during Carter's campaign. *left:* A view of Carter as representing both facets of the American people; *below:* A cynical view of Carter's altruism *Opposite:* Jimmy Carter laughs as a train interrupts his news conference at the Plains, Georgia, depot. Mrs. Lillian Carter is in the background

Reprinted with permission of Mike Peters, Dayton Daily Ne

Jimmy
CARTER
for President

Left: Carter speaking a[t] religious gathering; *belo[w]* Conspicuous support fo[r] Carter in his small hometown, Plains, Geor[gia]

Lawrence Smith, Columbus Ledger-Enquirer

Chris Harris, Gamma/Liaison

PLAINS, GEORGIA
HOME OF
JIMMY CARTE[R]
OUR NEXT PRESIDEN[T]

CARTER'S WHSE

running; and 36 hours later, Humphrey, with tears in his eyes, announced that he would not enter the race as an active candidate (though he would still be around in case his party called). Udall was hanging in there, but he had yet to win a primary. Carter went on to defeat favorite-son Lloyd Bentson in Texas and to win a resounding victory in his home state (83% of the vote), where not too long ago there had been those who said he couldn't get elected dogcatcher. These victories had been foreshadowed by Carter's earlier wins over Wallace in Florida and North Carolina. As Carter demonstrated that he did indeed have a chance of making it to the White House, the South began to rise up in support.

Again Carter was riding high, but again he suffered setbacks. As he was busy gathering endorsements from various elements of the party, two new candidates entered the primary course and dealt him defeats. Senator Frank Church beat him in Nebraska, and California Governor Jerry Brown beat him in Maryland. Brown won a sweeping victory in Maryland's "beauty contest," gathering votes from whites and blacks, rich and poor, conservatives and liberals. He was able to do so because he had the backing of the state political machine. (In Baltimore, for example, Governor Marvin Mandel swung black leaders behind Brown.) Brown was also a good campaigner. As a "new face" in the race, he seemed an attractive candidate. In a news conference, Carter even described Brown as "the new me." Still, although Brown won the popular vote in Maryland, he did not get any delegates, and in other states in which he planned to run he would have to stage difficult write-in campaigns.

Even in Michigan, where Carter had the backing of the

United Auto Workers and black Detroit Mayor Coleman Young, he did not get the big win he had expected. Instead he beat Udall by a dangerously narrow margin; he polled 44% of the vote to Udall's 42%.[25] Carter did well among the United Auto Workers (a large percentage of whom were white Southerners and blacks and probably would have supported Carter anyway without union leader Leonard Woodcock's endorsement); Udall did better among the other unions. Carter also scored heavily among blacks, winning two-thirds of the black vote, which had been his mainstay in other states. He was successful among fellow Protestants, too. But the fact remained that Udall had proved a serious challenger in Michigan. The Arizona senator particularly criticized Carter's fuzziness on the issues, and thus revealed a weak spot in his rival's camp.

The Nebraska, Maryland, and Michigan primaries showed that the "stop" movement was not dead yet. In the remaining primaries Carter would face one-to-one duels with Brown, Church, and Udall in different states. It was the kind of strategy that might have stopped Carter earlier on. By this time, however, he had such a strong lead in pledged delegates that it was questionable what a stop movement, no matter how strong, could do. But just in case Carter stumbled at the last minute, Humphrey, the darling of many liberals who still couldn't accept Carter, was waiting in the wings.

In the end the long-distance runner from Plains, Georgia, made it to the wire with a big win in the important Ohio primary. In Ohio Carter again did well among blacks (the black vote was 9.1% of the total, 39% in Cleveland, 12% in Columbus, and 11.3% in Dayton). He also made

sudden inroads into a core of voters that had supported
Udall in other primaries — liberal, Jewish, affluent
Democrats. Carter's supporters included one-half of the
Ohioans who had voted for George McGovern in 1972, as
well as one-half of the Democrats who had defected from
the party to vote for Nixon in '72. A survey of voter
attitudes showed that personal qualities, bandwagon
psychology, and the limited appeal of Carter's opponents
were all factors in his victory.[26]

In the wake of Carter's Ohio victory, the old king-
maker, Mayor Daley of Chicago, came out in support of
him. George Wallace, the giant Carter had slain back in
Florida, endorsed him now. Jackson freed his delegates to
Carter, and Church and Udall conceded. Humphrey
walked out on stage and took a final bow before retiring.
Only Brown remained in the running, but he could
scarcely pose a serious threat to Carter now. Not all of the
Democrats were happy with Carter, but they had to
acknowledge that he had emerged the winner. Throughout the campaign, Carter had been careful not to attack
the other candidates to the degree that it would be impossible for them to support him later on. He had courted
Daley from the beginning, refusing to contest Daley's
Cook County delegates during the Illinois primary, and
keeping in touch with the Mayor by phone. He had also
made phone calls to Humphrey, Udall, Jackson, and
Wallace just to be sure there were no hard feelings. Thus
a month before the 1976 Democratic Convention, Carter
was assured of a first-ballot nomination.

Watching Carter's meteoritic rise from a long-shot
candidate to the virtual Democratic nominee, many political commentators found themselves asking, "What does

it all mean?" They compared Carter's emergence to that of Wendell Wilkie in 1940 and John Kennedy in 1960. However, Carter had neither the financial backing that Wilkie had, nor the prior political exposure of Kennedy. He was simply different.

Carter's candidacy had been made possible by certain changes in the political system. McGovern had been the first dark-horse candidate to benefit from the increased number of primaries, instituted after 1968; Carter was the second. An outsider to the Democratic party establishment, he took his case directly to the people by running in 30 of the 31 primaries. From the time he announced his candidacy, a period of two years, he traveled approximately 400,000 miles and made around 2,000 speeches. Financially, he was able to make this all-out effort because of the new availability of Federal Matching Grants. In the end his success was remarkable: he won 17 of the 31 primaries and picked up at least 1,100 delegates in the process. Polls indicated that Humphrey might have won if he had entered the race, but the Happy Warrior chose to remain on the sidelines, ready to step in if the time seemed right. In '76, however, this type of strategy was no longer valid, for the campaign established an important precedent: in order to be considered, a candidate had to run in the primaries. Never had so many people had a chance to make a choice as they did in 1976, and Carter's victory reflected this fact.

In a number of states, Carter's black support had been an important element in his victory. His strong showing among blacks also had implications for the general election in November. In 1964 blacks had voted overwhelmingly for Lyndon Johnson, carrying him to a landslide victory over Barry Goldwater. The same thing could well happen for Carter in 1976.

Carter's candidacy had also become the rallying point for Southerners — not only in the Southern states, but also in other states like California, Ohio, Michigan, and Pennsylvania where black and white Southerners had migrated. Although the South was less of a distinct region than in the past, regional consciousness remained alive. Now after a hundred years of bitterness and disappointment, the South could once again hold its head up with pride. The leader so often dreamed of had finally come.

Throughout the campaign, Carter had demonstrated an ability to appeal to a wide spectrum of voters — black and white, young and old, blue collar and white collar, McGovern supporters and Nixon supporters. That he was able to do so testified to the success of his strategy. He steered a middle course, avoiding extremes on either side, and in some cases shifting his ground slightly when it was to his advantage to do so. He did not try to stir up old fires or build new ones; rather he sought to heal and unify.

Yet in Carter's effort to show that he was for everybody, he risked giving the impression that he was for no one, that he stood for nothing. He based his campaign on openness and honesty, yet to many he remained something of an enigma. There was little doubt in anyone's mind that he was a highly skilled politician, but as for what he would do if elected, that was another story. Still, he spoke to a sense of disillusionment with government that went deep into the American psyche; and he seemed to offer something that the others didn't — qualities of moral leadership which had been sadly lacking in the past. As Carter had correctly divined, voters in 1976 were more concerned with a candidate's character than they were with his positions on the issues.

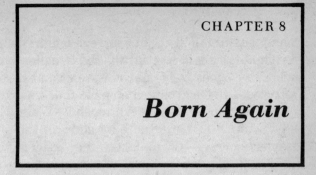

CHAPTER 8

Born Again

What does a Southern Baptist have in common with a Northern Protestant, Catholic, or Jew? This was an important question raised about Jimmy Carter during the '76 presidential campaign. Carter's religion came to the fore during the North Carolina primary. In response to questions from newsmen, Carter revealed, "In 1967, I had a profound religious experience that changed my life . . . I accepted Christ into my life." With this admission Carter opened the Pandora's box of problems about the place of religion in politics — a box that hadn't been opened since 1960 when John F. Kennedy ran for president. At that time many people wondered what would happen to the relation of church and state with a Roman Catholic chief executive.

However, the problem was different for Carter than it was for Kennedy, and not simply because Kennedy was a Roman Catholic and Carter a Baptist. The difference was that whereas Kennedy was not particularly devout, Carter was. It was the very sincerity of his religious beliefs that troubled people. As Garry Wills put it: "There is a concern over Carter's religion that is not mere bigotry.

135

It may seem unjust to punish real religion when we reward empty religiosity; but the thing makes sense. When Birch Bayh goes to his native hamlet and says he never feels closer to God than when he is there, we do not care because we know he does not mean it. When Nixon used Billy Graham to bless the billy clubs of the sixties, the insincerity gave us at least the relief of mockery. Kennedy's Catholicism was made up of gestures. But when a man *means* what he says in his awesome area, he drifts outside the ties and shared weaknesses that keep us in touch with each other."[1]

In particular, what seemed to set Carter apart from other poor, struggling mortals in the country was his complete lack of doubt. Asked by Bill Moyers if he ever had any doubts about himself, about God, or about life, Carter replied:

I can't think of any. I, obviously, don't know all the answers to philosophical questions and theological questions — the kind of questions that are contrived, but the things that I haven't been able to answer in a theory or supposition, I just accept them, and go on. Things that I can't influence or change.

I do have, obviously, many doubts about the best way to answer a question. Or to alleviate a concern. Or how to meet a need, or how to create in my own life a more meaningful purpose, and to let my life be expanded, in my heart and mind. So doubts about the best avenue to take among many options is a kind of doubt that is a constant presence with me.

But doubt about my faith — no. Doubt about my purpose of life — I don't have any doubts about that.[2]

Carter never doubted his religion. He grew up in a part of the country that, in the words of one Southerner, has "never ceased being haunted by God." At the age of 10 or so, he joined the local Baptist church, an act which represented not so much deliberate choice on his part as the accepted thing to do in a rural Southern community. At 18 he taught Sunday school classes like his father before him, and later on became a deacon of the church. When he went away to Annapolis, he took his faith with him. A classmate of his at the Naval Academy recalled that while many of the other cadets tried to get out of going to chapel, Jimmy went regularly to the local Baptist church in town, where he and another cadet volunteered to teach Sunday school classes. Jimmy had a class of ten-year-old girls, and since the admiral's daughter was one of them, he was invited to have lunch with the admiral and his family every Sunday. While at Annapolis, Carter went through the usual college sophomore debates "about why we are here, who made us, where we should go, what's our purpose."[3] Nevertheless, he emerged from these debates with his faith intact.

His religion never left him, but at one point he did have serious doubts about himself and his purpose in life. This was shortly after he had lost the first gubernatorial race in 1966. Of this period he said, "I wasn't getting any satisfaction out of any successes and when I had failures it was very upsetting. Even the smallest failures seemed like calamities to me. Life had no purpose."[4] Depressed and seeking meaning, Carter went for a long walk in the woods with his Evangelist sister, Ruth Carter Stapleton. His sister had herself emerged from a period of deep depression when she was able to experience God as a God of love. Ruth asked him if he would give up his life and everything he owned for Christ, and he said he would. But when she asked him if he would be able to give up politics, he had to think for a long time before finally answering that he would not. His sister told him that he would never find peace until he was able to do this. She remembered him as being very emotional and crying, but he had no such memory.

As a result of the talk with his sister, Carter had a "conversion experience." What was the nature of this experience? E. Brooks Holified, professor of American religious history at Emory University, offered this general description: "For these revivalistic Baptists — and for Carter — the conversion experience was neither a new revelation from God (which would diminish Biblical authority) nor a mystical absorption into the divine, but rather an experience of forgiveness, an undeserved gift, deeply felt and described in highly personal terms as a 'relationship with Christ.' Their 'rebirth' also entailed responsibilities; it initiated a process of personal growth designed to impose control over such passions as anger, lust, pride and fear, and to elicit the more positive virtues of love and compassion."[5]

Holified's description is in accord with various statements made by Carter in his autobiography and elsewhere. To Bill Moyers he said:

> I thought I was really a great Christian. And one day the preacher gave this sermon. I don't remember a thing he said. I just remember the title . . . "If You Were Arrested for Being A Christian — Would There Be Any Evidence to Convict You?"

And my answer by the time the sermon was over was "No." I never had really committed myself totally to God. My Christian beliefs were superficial. They were based primarily on pride. I never had done much for other people. I was always thinking about myself. And I changed somewhat for the better. I formed a much more intimate relationship with Christ. . . .[6]

In the wake of his conversion experience, Carter increased the extent of his service to his church. He realized he said, that during the three-month 1966 campaign he had made over 300,000 "visits" for himself, while in the past 14 years he made only 140 "visits" for Christ. He began to travel to various parts of Georgia and as far afield as Pennsylvania and Massachusetts to witness for Christ among those who had not yet received Christ into their lives. At one point he did religious and social work in a slum area in San Juan, Puerto Rico, and in the heat of the 1970 campaign, took off a week to work at a Baptist mission in an Atlanta slum.

Carter did not make the decision to follow his sister Ruth in a total commitment to life as an Evangelist; instead he viewed his political activity as a form of ministry. (He had once compared his state senate district to a "church with 80,000 members.") He was aware of his own tendency to "exalt" himself and "to dwell on the weaknesses and mistakes of others," and sought to overcome this tendency by expressing love for his fellow man as a demonstration of his love for Christ. In his autobiography he writes, "I have come to realize that in every person there is something fine and pure and noble, along with a desire for self-fulfillment. Political and religious leaders must attempt to provide a society within which these human attributes can be nurtured and enhanced."[7]

Observing Carter during the '76 presidential campaign, most agreed that he was an extremely ambitious man. Carter, claimed, however, that his ambition and drive were channeled towards the achievement of constructive goals. As he told Bill Moyers, "I feel like I have one life to live — I feel like that God wants me to do the best I can with it. And that's quite often my major prayer — Let me live my life so that it will be meaningful."[8]

Carter's record as governor would seem to bear out his claim that he is not motivated solely by a desire to advance himself. He pushed for things like prison reform, civil rights, and programs for the handicapped. In short, his administration was very much a champion of the weak and the poor. E. Brooks Holified writes, "His [Carter's] sermons to professional associations usually excoriated their collective selfishness and called for expansion of their services. He rarely used the word 'God' in his official speeches, but, when he did, the term functioned generally in two ways: the poor should have the right and means to develop their 'God-given talents,' and the powerful have the responsibility to share their 'God-given blessings' for the common welfare." Holified also observed that "Carter persuaded his own fashionable Northside Drive Baptist Church to set up medical clinics in Atlanta ghettos."[9]

As for the specific content of Carter's religious beliefs, he is not a Fundamentalist. His social activism distinguishes him from the Fundamentalists and their doctrine of "premillenial dispensationalism." That doctrine states simply that there is no point in trying to do anything to better the world before Christ's imminent return. Also,

Carter does not share the complete certainty of the Fundamentalists. He quotes the liberal Protestant theologian Paul Tillich to the effect "that religion is a search for the relationship between us and God, and us and our fellow human beings," and "that when we quit searching, in effect, we've lost our religion." For Carter this means that "When we become self-satisfied, proud, sure — at that point we lose the self-searching, the humility, the subservience to God's will . . . ."[10]

Carter may agree with certain Fundamentalist doctrines, but this does not necessarily mean that he takes the entire Bible literally. He has said, "I find it difficult to question Holy Scripture, but I admit that I do have trouble with Paul sometimes, especially when he says that a woman's place is with her husband, and that she should keep quiet and cover her head in church. I just can't go along with him on that."[11]

Broadly speaking, Evangelism does represent an anti-intellectual streak in American life, according to the American historian, Richard Hofstader. And today there are those who question how an intelligent person can talk about Jesus. As Gonzo journalist Hunter S. Thompson writes, "I have never felt comfortable around people who talk about their feelings for Jesus, or any other deity for that matter, because they are usually none too bright . . . . Or maybe 'stupid' is a better way of saying it. . . ."[12] Yet Thompson also describes Carter as one of the most intelligent politicians he has ever met, and there are certainly others who would concur in his judgment. Carter manages to combine the sharp intelligence of a nuclear engineer with a deep religious faith.

Writer and columnist Garry Wills has taken Carter to

task for the narrowness of his religious faith. Wills writes, "He [Carter] is a man who reads the Bible every day, and has taught it all his adult life. I asked him if he ever entertained, in Sunday school classes or private study, the "form criticism" of the New Testament. 'What is that?' he asked. A bit dumbfounded, I said, 'The kind of textual analysis Rudolf Bultmann did.' He knew that name, but could not remember if he had read anything by Bultmann. For a bright and educated modern man, dealing with the thing he says matters most to him, he shows an extraordinarily reined-in curiosity. It suggests a kind of willed narrowness of mastery."[13]

However, Carter has never claimed to be a theologian. He has read Reinhold Niebuhr, some Tillich, some Soren Kierkegaard, and some Dietrich Bonhoeffer, but he is no expert on theological matters. According to E. Brooks Holifield, one of Carter's former ministers said "that Carter was not really interested in theological issues," and "that religion for him was basically a matter of inward piety and 'loving your neighbor.' "[14]

Still, Carter stands above other politicians like Lyndon Johnson and George Wallace who used the Evangelical idiom. Catholic theologian Michael Novak has written that "neither man [Johnson or Wallace] could achieve the education, the polish, the class of Jimmy Carter. As Billy Graham towers above other evangelists in his smoothness and modern ways, so also Jimmy Carter's speech has an almost flawless deftness. He has a cosmopolitan way. He speaks for the national superculture, not just for a subculture."[15]

During the '76 campaign, Carter's role as spokesman for the Evangelist "national superculture" was apparent.

What was the size of this constituency? Michael Novak has estimated that there are at least 40 million Evangelical Protestants in America; others set the figure at 50 million. The growing popularity of the movement is indicated by the skyrocketing sales of Billy Graham's latest book, *Angels: God's Secret Agents*, which reached the 1.3 million mark in a period of a few months. Evangelists are not only located in the Bible Belt. They are spread all over the United States. The movement is strong in California, Oregon, and Washington; and there are also many Evangelists in such states as Iowa, New Hampshire, Massachusetts, Florida, North Carolina, Wisconsin, and upstate New York. Evangelists in these states and some others were an important source of support for Carter during the presidential primaries.

Yet in the '76 campaign, Carter also had to deal with opposition from ethnic groups in the Northeastern industrial states, to whom his Southern Baptist heritage was completely alien. He had to convince them that he was not a redneck religious bigot who claimed a hotline to God. It was obvious, for instance, that Carter prayed a lot, "in church, and even at home and while campaigning, for Pete's sake."[16] He said he prayed to God at least 25 times a day, and that when he was governor he had spent many hours on his knees in a small private room next to his office. What did he pray about? He said that he had never asked God to let him be president. "I ask God to let me do what's right, and to let me do what's best, that my life be meaningful, in an optimum way, and if I win or lose, I believe I can accept the decision with composure . . . ."[17] How did he know God's will? Carter said ". . . when I have a sense of peace, and just self-assurance — I don't know where it comes from — but what I'm doing is a right thing — I assume, maybe, in an unwarranted way that that's doing God's will."[18]

But these explanations by no means satisfied everyone. The Jews, in particular, were concerned about Carter's religion. After all, he came from a state where in 1915 a Northern Jew was found guilty of murder and lynched by an angry mob, in which there were undoubtedly more than a few Southern Baptists. At the most extreme were some who were afraid that God might suddenly tell Carter to exterminate the Jews; others worried that under a Carter presidency the Jews would be relegated to the status of second-class citizens. With regard to foreign policy, Jews wondered if they could trust a born-again Baptist to continue the United States' policy of support to Israel.

Carter took pains to assure Jewish voters that he was on their side in terms of the situation in the Middle East, that he was not prejudiced, and that he would maintain a strict separation of church and state if elected. He was able to attract some Jewish support, mainly among the leaders of the Jewish community in Atlanta (for whom his religion had never posed a problem in the first place). Later on in the primary race, Mayor Abraham Beame of New York endorsed Carter; he also had the support of Morris Abram, a former Georgian and New York lawyer, who was chairman of the Moreland Act Commission on Nursing Homes. In an article entitled "Carter and Baptists," which appeared in the *New York Times*, Abram noted that Carter as governor had appointed a Jew as chairman of the Board of Regents of the Georgia university system — something which was unheard of previously. Abram also pointed out that Roger Williams, founder of the Baptist Church, was the father of religious toleration as well. He concluded:"I do not claim that Jimmy Carter knows all the nuances of American pluralism. But on his record, and knowing him, I believe he wants to learn. Nothing that has happened in the months of his Presidential campaign has changed my mind."[19]

Rabbi Marc H. Tanenbaum, national director of interreligious affairs for the American Jewish Committee, addressed the problem in a statement sent out to Jewish leaders all over the country, entitled, "Carter, Evangelism and Jews." Rabbi Tanenbaum raised the questions: "Is Jimmy Carter good for the Jews?" and "Is Jimmy Carter good for America?" He did not, however, attempt to answer these questions; rather he urged caution in allowing religious considerations to affect voting. "What most Northerners do not understand," he wrote, "is that there is today a pluralism of theologies as well as social values among evangelists, as there is among Catholics and Jews . . . . And there are new evangelicals who are committed to social justice as passionately as any Northerner. The point of this message is not to presume to tell you whom to vote for, but to [urge you] to do your homework, and not vote on the basis of prejudice, mythologies, and stereotypes."[20]

A voter who did his homework would discover that as governor of Georgia Carter had maintained a strict separation of church and state. He did away with the rather ostentatious religious service, which had been held each day in the state house under the previous governor, Lester Maddox. He also secured legislation giving 18-year-olds full citizenship rights, including the right to buy liquor — an act which drew forth the wrath of several Southern Baptist clergymen. Before this, when he was a state senator, Carter voted against a proposed requirement in the new state constitution that said that God must be worshipped in Georgia. Carter preferred the wording in the Bill of Rights which guaranteed freedom of religion. (In the 1970 campaign his vote in this instance was used to show that he was an atheist.)

Carter has said that he would not use the presidency as a pulpit, and his record as governor certainly suggests that he wouldn't. What then would Carter's religion mean in terms of his presidency? Carter thinks he will make a better president because of his religion, and there are those who definitely agree. William Lee Miller, author of *Piety Along the Potomac* and director of the Poynter Center at Indiana University, observed that "the political fallout from the [Carter's] religious belief is likely not to be an avoidance of, but an encouragement to, social justice and sympathy with the poor."[21] In a similar vein, Hal Gulliver, editor of the *Atlanta Constitution*, writes:

> Carter is no saint, nor is he a religious fanatic, nor is he unaware (as he has taken some pains to stress) that there are lines of distinction between personal faith and conviction and public policies and the public responsibilities of a President. But he is, again, a genuinely religious man, one who believes in good and in evil and that you are measured finally at the end of life by your efforts to be on the side of good.
>
> What does that mean in terms of a President? Well, I think it means a profound caring about people and about what happens to them and about dealing with

them honestly and being concerned about what
government does or does not do as it affects individuals. . . .[22]

There is little doubt that Carter's vision of what government should be is presented in distinctly christian
terms. In his autobiography he writes, "Government at
all levels can be competent, economical and efficient. Yet
I would hasten to point out that nowhere in the Constitution of the United States, or the Declaration of Independence, or the Bill of Rights, or the Emancipation Procla-
mation, or the Old Testament or the New Testament do
you find the words "economy" or "efficiency." Not that
these two words are unimportant. But you discover other
words like *honesty, integrity, fairness, liberty, justice,
courage, patriotism, compassion, love* — and many
others which describe what a human being ought to be.
These are also the same words which describe what a
government of human beings ought to be."[23]

In his '76 campaign speeches, Carter frequently said
that what he wanted to see was "a government as filled
with love as the American people." He also just about as
often quoted Reinhold Niebuhr to the effect that "politics
is the sad art of establishing justice in a sinful world." The
two visions are somewhat contradictory, but they,
nevertheless, exist side by side in Carter's thinking. In
the Law Day Address, which was given at the University
of Georgia in May, 1974, and which so impressed "outlaw"
journalist Hunter S. Thompson, Carter showed his appreciation of Niebuhr's thinking. The speech was about
law and justice, and in it Carter attacked lawyers, judges,
and the entire criminal justice system for allowing the
rich and the powerful to get off scot-free, while the poor

are punished. He agreed with Niebuhr that owing to man's sinful nature, the perfect society could never be established here on earth, but he cited Martin Luther King, Jr., as an example of a man struggling to achieve justice in a far from perfect world.

The Law Day speech and Carter's references to Niebuhr elsewhere showed that he is not so naive as to believe that love is enough. As Neibuhr pointed out, Christ loved, and ended up being crucified. Carter's Protestant piety makes him optimistic about the country's future, but at the same time he is aware of Niebuhrian limits in terms of what can actually be accomplished. He understands power and its abuses, but wants it because ". . . I'd like to have a chance to change things that I don't like, and to correct inequities as I discern them, and to be a strong spokesman for those that are not strong. . . ."[24] He is a born-again Baptist who believes in Jesus and love, but he is also a politician seeking to establish justice in a sinful world.

CHAPTER 9

The Private Man

"There's another Jimmy out there in the world," his mother, Miss Lillian Carter observed during the '76 presidential campaign. She added that it was sometimes hard for her to realize that the candidate she saw on her TV screen was her son. Her remark brought up the question of what Carter was like offstage. What about the private man behind the public figure?

While Carter's broad grin became the butt of many jokes during the presidential race, he cracked few jokes himself. This set some people to wondering whether, in fact, he possessed a sense of humor. Carter's mother, his wife, and his adviser, Charles Kirbo, all insisted that Carter did have a sense of humor, but that there wasn't much opportunity for it to surface during the campaign. Said his wife Rosalynn, "Jimmy has a great sense of humor. People just don't know that about him yet."[1] But examples of the Carter brand of humor were not forthcoming. To Sally Quinn of the *Washington Post* Carter said, "I don't think I'm a funny person, but I can see the humor of things when they happen. I don't consciously search for puns. What's funny to me are W.C. Fields

149

movies. . . . I respond well to jokes on me. I'm very teaseable. My wife doesn't like to tease anybody though and she doesn't like to be teased. My sons and I tease each other all the time."[2] A reporter covering Carter observed that his was a ". . . wry, self-deprecating sense of humor . . ." but that it was ". . . often submerged by his single-minded commitment to his goals. . . ."[3]

Carter showed himself to be an extremely hard-working man both as governor and as a campaigner, but was his life all work and no play? Bill Moyers put the question to him: "What do you do . . . for fun?" Carter's reply: ". . . when I get home I change immediately into work clothes, put on brogans and dungarees — and either go to the farm, walk in the woods, — my wife and I like to hunt arrowheads. We go out in the fields as they've been plowed and rained on, and we walk sometimes for hours just talking to each other about different things, sometimes politics — right often about our family. . . ."[4]

Carter's mother painted a picture of him as relaxed and "happy-go-lucky" when he was at home in Plains on the weekends during the campaign. She said he went around bare-footed and played Frisbee out in the yard. "He's a normal good sport," she commented.

In his autobiography Carter includes "canoeist" in the list of his various vocations and avocations — farmer, businessman, nuclear physicist, etc. While he was governor, he and Rosalynn made one- and two-day trips to various wilderness areas in the state:

We rode the wild rivers in rafts, canoes, and kayaks. We panned successfully for gold in a remote North

Georgia stream. We studied the wildlife programs on our isolated game preserves, and inspected the virgin cypress groves on Lewis Island in the mouth of the Altamaha River.

Our favorite place was Cumberland Island, off the Southeast Georgia coast, where one can see dozens of sea turtles coming ashore to lay their eggs in the early summer. We would watch the sun rise over the Atlantic, and drive down twenty miles of the broad white beach without seeing another living soul.[5]

Carter's favorite spectator sport is stock car racing. In an interview with Sally Quinn, he said,

"I've been a fan for the last 30 years. When I was in the Navy in New York, Rosy and I used to go to the dirt tracks in northern New York. Then back in Georgia we used to drive down to Sebring and stay in the back of our station wagon for a few days. We'd go to Daytona a lot too. We know all the race-car drivers. When I was governor we had a banquet at the mansion every year for all the race car drivers. I don't know why I like it. I don't like to drive fast myself. I used to study different cars. I have records of automobile engines that I listen to. We know all the pit crews and the engineers. Sometimes we visit the pit crews during the races.[6]

For relaxation Carter also reads a great deal. His favorite authors include two Southerners — James Agee and William Faulkner — and the Welsh poet, Dylan Thomas. Dmitri Shostakovich is one of his favorite composers, and he also likes the music of Bob Dylan. He quotes from Dylan songs in his autobiography and in some of his speeches. When Carter was governor, Bob Dylan was a guest at the governor's mansion. Of his relationship with Dylan, Carter has said, "I really like rock music and Bob Dylan and I get along really well. He's very, very shy. Painfully so."[7] He is on friendly terms with rock star Gregg Allman, too. About both Allman and Dylan, people whose life-styles are very different from his own, Carter commented, "I care for these people and I respect them. . . . They are strange kids and yet they look on me with love. There's a closeness I feel to these young people."[8]

Perhaps the strangest of all is Carter's relationship with the "outlaw" journalist Hunter S. Thompson. During the '76 campaign Thompson, with his usual "fear and loathing," endorsed Carter in a long, rambling piece that appeared in *Rolling Stone*. Thompson first met Carter in 1974 at a Law Day ceremony honoring Dean Rusk at the University of Georgia. Throughout the event, Thompson made frequent trips out to the parking lot where he had a bottle stashed in the trunk of a secret serviceman's car. But when Carter began to speak, he was so impressed with what he heard that he abandoned the bottle in favor of his tape recorder. Since then Thompson spent a fair amount of time with Carter, whom he describes as "one of the most intelligent politicians I've ever met, and also one of the strangest."[9] In particular, Carter's "Jesus talk" makes Thompson feel uncomfortable. How comfortable many politicians feel around Dr. Thompson, who is notorious for his bizarre ravings under the influence, is another question. However, in Carter's case, Thompson writes: "Both Carter and his wife have always been amazingly tolerant of my behavior, and on one or two occasions they have had to deal with me in a noticeably bent condition. I have always been careful not to commit any felonies right in front of them, but other than that I have never made much of an effort to adjust my behavior around Jimmy Carter or anyone else in his family—including his 78-year-old mother, Miss Lillian, who is the only member of the Carter family I could comfortably endorse for the presidency, right now, with no reservations at all."[10]

Carter's own life-style is obviously very different from Thompson's. Those who don't agree with everything Carter has done in public life, nevertheless affirm that his personal life is above reproach. During the '76 campaign, his mother told the story of a reporter from the *National Enquirer* who visited her every day for a week in an effort to find out something bad that Jimmy had done as a child. Unfortunately for the reporter, she couldn't come up with anything. "He's been a lot of places and withstood a lot of temptations," she said, though she admitted that sometimes she wished her son had done something a little off-color — if only because it would make a better story.

Still, Carter is by no means a saint. He enjoys his Scotch, and he has also been known to use profanity on occasion. On the subject of Richard Nixon, he once told a reporter, "I despise the bastard, but I pray that he will find peace."[11] He can throw a mean phrase when it comes to a political opponent; he once said that being called a liar by Lester Maddox was like being called ugly by a frog. He is not one to turn the other cheek, nor does he take defeat easily. His '76 campaign manager called him "the world's worst loser." Aides tend to make themselves scarce when their boss is in one of his tempers.

Carter is a tough guy, but he is also capable of great

tenderness and compassion. During the '76 campaign, the story of a newsman's daughter who was stricken with cancer brought tears to his eyes. The next day he dug up arrowheads in the fields behind his home in Plains, polished them, and mailed them to the newsman's daughter. "He's a very charismatic, spiritual man," said Bill Shipp, associate editor of the *Atlanta Constitution* and a former Sanders supporter.

In the '76 race, Carter spoke of a kind of communion he shared with voters. To Bill Moyers he said, "when I stand out on a factory shift line like I did this morning . . . everybody that comes through there, when I shake hands with them, for that instant, I really care about them in a genuine way. And I believe they know it a lot of times. Quite often I will shake hands with a woman who works in a plant, say an older woman, and I just touch her hand, and quite frequently they'll put their arms around my neck and say — God bless you, son or good luck . . ."[12]

Yet of all the candidates, Carter was the least personally accessible, and in his private life there are few who claim to know him well outside of his immediate family. He is a reserved and somewhat shy person, but it's also true that he doesn't seem to have the time to be close to many people. Said his press secretary, Jody Powell, ". . . His [Carter's] quotient for small talk was and is very low. If he can't get rid of the people he believes are wasting his time, he simply leaves the room himself, not physically, but mentally. He just turns the whole thing off and uses his time in a way he believes is more productive. . . ."[13]

However, Carter's family is important to him. He told Bill Moyers that "about the only thing I do now for fun is look forward to being home. I stay gone a lot. Away from

Plains, away from our house, away from our little daughter, away from my wife. Away from my mother and mother-in-law, and my brother and sister and my wife's kinfolks . . . we have very few moments alone, and so the fun in my life now is just re-establishing for a 24-hour period or 32-hour period, whatever it is, the structure of my family."[14]

It was the structure of his family that gave Carter's life stability as a child, and thus he recognizes the importance of maintaining that structure as an adult. His younger brother and sisters apparently look up to him and feel that he can do no wrong. His brother Billy, once described as a "closet redneck" by Hamilton Jordan, manages the family business in Carter's absence. One of his sisters, Gloria, is an artist and motorcycle enthusiast who lives with her peanut farmer husband, Walter Spann, near Plains. Gloria is interesting because she is the only one in the family to break out of the hard-working Carter mold. After a born-again experience, she decided that what she really wanted to do was quit working and stay at home and simply be a housewife. "Gloria is different," her mother comments.

Carter's youngest sister, Ruth Carter Stapleton, is a full-time Evangelist. According to her brother, she expresses "in the most refreshing way her deep faith and personal relationship with Christ."[15] She underwent a conversion experience a decade ago and since then has traveled around the country preaching and providing what she describes as a "healing of memories." Her approach combines spiritualism with psychotherapy. She calls on people to go back to traumatic moments in their past and inject Jesus with his love and forgiveness into these experiences.

Carter's mother is an equally dynamic woman, though in a more secular vein. She once said that one of the main reasons she went to church was the fact that there wasn't much else to do in Plains. After her husband's death, her search for things to do took her to the University of Alabama at Auburn, where she was a housemother for a fraternity for seven years. Tiring of this, she returned to Plains to operate a small hospital in a nearby town. Then one night she was watching television and saw an ad for the Peace Corps, which said that age was no barrier. In 1966, aged 68, she applied, was accepted, and spent two years in India working as a nurse.

Carter and his mother have a great deal of respect and admiration for each other, though they don't see eye to eye on everything. She was against the Vietnam War long before her son was. She also had her own ideas about what he should and shouldn't say in the '76 campaign. "I told him to quit that stuff about never telling a lie and being a Christian and how he loves his wife more than the day he met her. There are some things you don't have to go around saying."[16]

Carter and his wife have four children. The three boys — Jack, Chip and Jeff — are all grown-up and married. Each helped out in both the '70 and '76 campaigns. While Carter was governor, each worked in his office with him during different legislative sessions, serving without pay. The Carters' youngest child, Amy, was born after 21 years of marriage. Even she is involved in her father's political life. Asked by reporters in '76 if she thought her father would make a good president, she said "yes," but added that she didn't want him to be president because she didn't want to live in the White House. She also told reporters that she was going to travel with her father everywhere on the campaign trail — a plan that was rejected by the family because she was only eight years old. As a second-grader in an integrated school in Plains, Amy had 13 white classmates, 16 black classmates, a black teacher, and a white principal. (In the '76 campaign, Carter never failed to mention this fact when the question of his stand on busing to achieve racial integration came up.)

All of Carter's family have stumped for him at one point or another, but none has taken a more active part in his political life than his wife, Rosalynn. She has shown herself to be every bit as hard-working as any member of the Carter clan. Her father died when she was young, so her mother supported the family by working at the post office and sewing trousseaus. Rosalynn helped with the sewing and also worked in a beauty parlor. She got $4 a week for lunch and expenses. After graduating from high school, she went on to junior college in nearby Americus for two years before her marriage to Jimmy. When her husband left the navy and they returned to Plains, she helped out with the family business. She took part in the first campaign in '62; and when Jimmy was away in the state senate, she sometimes worked from 6 a.m. to 11 p.m. She stumped for Carter again in '66 and handled all his political correspondence between 1966 and 1969. Rosalynn was one of the few who encouraged him to make another try for the governorship in 1970. She was involved in all the strategy sessions, and she went on the campaign trail in '70.

When Carter was governor, Rosalynn headed the

Governor's Commission to Improve Services for the Mentally and Emotionally Handicapped. The commission was responsible for the establishment of 136 mental health centers all over the state. In the '76 campaign, she said that as First Lady she would continue to work for better care for the mentally ill. She was also concerned with improving day-care facilities, and she supported the Equal Rights Amendment.

An extremely shy person for whom campaigning was originally difficult, Rosalynn came into her own in the '76 effort. She campaigned by herself for the most part, following a strenuous schedule similar to her husband's. Carter considered her to be "a substitute candidate . . . a perfect extension of me."[17] Her social secretary and scheduler, Madeline MacBean, agreed: "We use her just like we use Jimmy. She has exactly the same schedule, only we send her where he cannot go."[18]

For the campaign Rosalynn carefully studied both Carter's record as governor and his positions on the various issues. But as for the actual campaigning, she followed her own instincts. "My husband has never told me what to say or not to say but if I think something could be harmful, I ask him about it."[19] The fact was that she did seem to know exactly what to say. She showed herself to be as adept as her husband at shaping her speech to a particular audience. Thus, in front of elderly audiences, she always mentioned Jimmy's mother, telling them what a wonderful woman she was and saying how she wished they could meet her. She was also quick to advise her husband to avoid controversial stands. At one point she called Carter to let him know that people were upset about his position on the mortgage interest deduction, which was part of his tax reform program. "I told him not to try to explain it," she said, "I told him to be simple and say,'I'm going to lower your taxes. I'm not going to take away your deduction.' He said, 'You're right.' "[20]

Rosalynn also made significant contributions to Carter's overall '76 strategy. She pushed for his running in every primary, and it was she who advised him to stay with his original plan of eliminating Wallace in the Florida primary, rather than trying to follow up his New England — New Hampshire victory with another one in Massachusetts. As it became evident later, Carter's win over the Alabama governor in Florida was one of the turning points of his campaign.

Carter obviously thinks highly of his wife's judgment. During the campaign, he said that if he was elected, Rosalynn could travel around the country for him talking to people and getting their views. She could also represent him abroad because she knows his positions and can listen to people. As he would be an activist president, she would be an activist First Lady.

Those who know them both agree that Rosalynn is every bit as tough-minded and ambitious as her husband. "She's as ambitious to be First Lady as she is for him to be president," an aide commented.[21] Rosalynn herself said, "I'm not doing this only for Jimmy — there are lots of things I can do as First Lady."[22] During the campaign, Rosalynn denied charges that her husband was cold and calculating. "He's a planner. I don't think you have to be cold and calculating to decide you're going to be president — and then lay out a plan for it. . . He never had time for frivolous things."[23] Yet she displayed the same humorless determination that her husband was taken to task for.

Carter's mother has said of Rosalynn, "I admire her, but I have never seen her let her hair down, never heard her tell a joke."[24] A certain amount of competition apparently exists between these two very dynamic women. An aide said, "One reason Rosalynn campaigns so hard is to show Jimmy she's as important to him as his mother."[25]

There is little question, however, that Rosalynn has a fair amount of influence over her husband. His mother said, "If I want Jimmy to do anything, I ask Rosalynn. She can do anything in the world with Jimmy and she's the only one. He listens to her. He thinks she has a great mind."[26]   Hamilton Jordan agreed, "If Jody [Carter's press secretary Jody Powell] and I strike out, the best thing to do is to try to get Rosalynn on our side."[27]

Rosalynn is also the only person who really knows Jimmy Carter well. "Nobody knows Jimmy intimately except his wife," a friend said; Carter's mother agreed, "He's secretive to everybody but his wife." What do they talk about when they're alone? Rosalynn said that relations weren't always harmonious during the campaign, that they had many arguments over issues. "I scream and he sits there and doesn't say anything."[28] What kinds of issues? Rosalynn wasn't telling because she didn't think a political campaign was the time to reveal disagreements.

For the time being, at least, there were aspects of the private man behind the public figure that remained in the shadows.

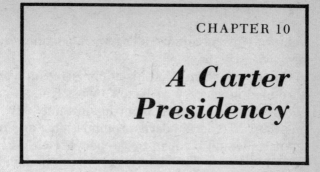

CHAPTER 10

A Carter Presidency

For many people a vote for Jimmy Carter for president requires a leap of faith. He's a mystery, a giant question mark in their minds. Nevertheless, certain things can be said regarding the qualities and type of experience Carter would bring to the job, the kinds of policies he would pursue, and his views of the presidency.

On the plus side, Carter has shown himself to be an extremely hard-working and intelligent man. He has a good grasp of details, and can handle complex problems. He also has a great deal of self-confidence, and this, he feels, would make him acceptable to the Eastern liberal establishment in a way that a previous Southern president, Lyndon Johnson, was not. ". . . I'm not sure that Johnson was ever sure of himself when he was President. . . ."[1] Carter told a *New York Times* reporter.

But what about moral qualities — could Carter give the country the kind of moral leadership that was lacking under the Nixon administration? Throughout his campaign, Carter presented himself to voters as a man of integrity who would not lie to the people in the way that Nixon did. He cited Harry Truman as his favorite president, saying he admired Truman's openness and frankness with the people.

Carter maintains that his administration would not be shrouded in secrecy as Nixon's was. He has proposed a comprehensive "government-in-sunshine" law, whereby meetings of federal boards, commissions, and regulatory agencies would be open to the people (with some exceptions); activities by lobbyists would be made public; "sweetheart" arrangements between industry and the regulatory agencies would be broken up; and business and financial involvements of all public officials (including the president) would be disclosed. He has also said that, with some exceptions, he would let the minutes of his cabinet meetings be made public, and that cabinet members would go before joint sessions of Congress to be examined and questioned about foreign affairs, defense, agriculture, and other matters. He would release a yearly audit of his personal finances (as he did during his term as governor), and he would be available to the news media. As governor, Carter held news conferences once a week and generally enjoyed good relations with the press. As president, he says he would hold news conferences every month or perhaps more frequently.

It seems reasonable to assume that Carter would do these things, as the general thrust of his administration as governor was toward opening up government to the people to a greater degree than was previously done. There remains, however, the problem of his promise never to tell a lie. During the campaign, Carter was attacked as a liar and political charlaton. His critics claimed to perceive in him the very Nixonian qualities of deviousness and lack of principle that Carter said he abhorred.

Undoubtedly, Carter is no boy scout. He is a politician and thus perfectly capable of exaggerating a little here, and trimming a little there. As David Nordan, political editor of the *Atlanta Journal*, writes, "Few instances can be found where Carter lied outright or seriously contradicted himself. But like most Georgia politicians, he is a master of the art of leaving his position sufficiently vague to allow everyone to hear what they wanted to hear."[2]

But does this mean that Carter has no positions, that he believes in nothing but himself, as Steven Brill and others have charged? Carter's record as governor clearly demonstrates that he does have concerns beyond that of simply furthering his own ambition. Of course, Steven Brill maintains that Carter only did good things as governor because he already had his eye on the presidency. This seems, however, to be an incredibly cynical reading of the man. It ignores his earlier efforts in the field of civil rights, and the fact that he expressed his concern for blacks and the poor and the weak at the very beginning of his administration in his Inaugural Address — before he had any thoughts of running for president.

If there is one thing which distinguishes Carter from a man like Nixon, it is his strong religious beliefs, the sincerity of which not even his harshest critics have questioned. He has frequently expressed his sense of responsibility toward his fellow man, and he acted upon that sense of responsibility as governor. There is no reason to believe that he would not do the same as president. He does seek power, but not as an end in itself. Rather he views it as a means of achieving his goals and helping those less powerful. He genuinely believes that a president should not lie to the people, though he admits that as President, "There will be times when I'm asked a question that I might refuse to answer. But if I give an answer, it will be the truth."[3]

Still, being a good and decent man is no guarantee of success as a president. Carter lacks a Washington background, but this is not necessarily a handicap. Traditionally, Americans have looked to governors as having the kind of administrative experience important for a president. It has only been recently that presidents have come from the ranks of Congress. As governor, Carter had to deal with some of the same problems faced by the federal government, though on a much smaller scale. He was also on the receiving end of federal programs, so he has some understanding of how the federal bureaucracy works and doesn't work. But whether Carter could streamline the federal government as he did state government is another matter, given the magnitude of the bureaucracy and the complexity of problems involved.

Carter's experience in the conduct of foreign affairs is limited. During his travels as governor, he met with various foreign leaders. He was also a member of the Trilateral Commission, consisting of high officials of Japan, Western Europe, and the United States. He reportedly took an active part in a commission session in Tokyo, revealing his grasp of the problems of non-Communist countries. Nevertheless, as he himself acknowledges, foreign affairs is not his strong point. He would have to depend on help from his advisers in this area. Yet here, as with the conduct of national affairs, experience with recent presidents has tended to indicate that perhaps the character of the leader is more important than any specific credentials.

The kind of staff Carter would bring with him to the White House is important too. Albert R. Hunt of the *Wall Street Journal* describes Carter's staff (now jokingly referred to as the "Georgia Mafia") as "a group of bright Southern charmers, people unfamiliar with the ways of Washington but possessed with shrewd instincts and unafraid of confrontation."[4] He also calls them "pragmatists," who like Carter "seem interested chiefly in what works, or sells."[5] However, he notes a major difference in personality between Carter and his staff: "While he's serious, sober and a bit self-righteous, they are fun-loving and irreverent."[6]

In the '76 campaign, Carter and his staff came under some attack for their attitude toward the press. In an article appearing in the *National Journal*, Robert Walters writes, "Virtually unnoticed in the turmoil of the contest for this year's Democratic presidential nomination has been the animosity evidenced by former Georgia Gov. Jimmy Carter, the leader in that race, toward the news media.

"Carter and his staff have become increasingly testy with reporters, especially those engaged in investigative reporting about the candidate and his campaign — journalists with a penchant for noting the contradictory positions he has taken on numerous issues and others who press for answers to tough questions."[7] Walter gives examples of several newsmen who complained of bad experiences with the Carter staff, among them one Washington reporter who said, "The Carter people have the attitude of 'you're either for us or you're against us.' If you're a reporter who asks tough questions, that means you're against them. They then respond with unnecessary, juvenile abrasiveness, a la Ron Ziegler. They have a minor league approach to dealing with the press."[8]

But this opinion was not shared by all reporters covering Carter. *Washington Post* reporter David Broder, who certainly cannot be classified as pro-Carter, wrote at the time of the Oregon primary, "On the Democratic side, what Oregon showed was that Jimmy Carter's staff has survived the ups and downs of his 16-month campaign with its energy and sense of humor intact — not a bad recommendation. Their courtesy and hospitality are unfailing, even to critical reporters, and they have miraculously not begun to inhale their own success."[9] Broder also commented on what he considered to be the attractive qualities of the Carter entourage: "a relaxed, irreverent and easy relationship with the candidate, sustained by a strong admiration for him as a man and a politician."[10]

Still, there are those who claim that the Carter staff is overly dedicated to their boss, that, in fact, they believe in nothing but him. Here again the Nixon analogy appears. However, Carter staffers insist that while they are loyal to Carter, they are not to be compared with the Nixon people because of their higher personal standards. They also argue that a Palace Guard situation could never develop because Carter consults with a number of others besides the three considered closest to him — Hamilton Jordan, executive secretary when Carter was governor and '76 campaign manager; press secretary Jody Powell; and Atlanta lawyer, Charles Kirbo. The others on the staff from whom Carter seeks advice include campaign treasurer Robert Lipshutz, an Atlanta lawyer; Gerald Rafshoon, Carter's advertising manager; pollster Patrick

Caddell; Stuart Eizenstat, another Atlanta lawyer and head of the '76 issues staff; Peter Bourne, chief of the Washington office, and his wife Mary, who say they represent the liberal element of the party closest to Carter. A non-staffer who could be expected to have some influence is Congressman Andrew Young, whose support was important to Carter in the '76 campaign.

Judging from Carter's record as governor, it is fair to assume that he would reach out beyond his immediate staff for advice on matters of policy. He says he would find high-caliber people to serve in his Cabinet and would deal with them directly rather than through his staff. "I wouldn't want my Cabinet going through staff members for important decisions," he says. "I don't like to administer through top staff people."[11]

Yet even with the best of advisers, could Carter — a man who has lived most of his life in one part of the country — be an effective leader of a pluralistic society? Steven Brill, who is otherwise highly critical of Carter, acknowledges that Carter's "two years of house-to-house campaigning will probably have taught him more about the country than most Presidents ever know."[12] Carter confesses that he is not "completely at home with all elements of a pluralistic society," but thinks that his "background would be equivalent to many people who have become president, who have served successfully."[13]

There is also the possibility that Carter as a Southerner could make certain unique contributions to the national life if he were elected president. In a book called *The Burden of Southern History*, C. Vann Woodward distinguishes at least four positive characteristics of the South, which in his view set it apart from the rest of the country.

He contrasts Southern poverty with American plenty, Southern defeat and disappointment with American success, Southern guilt and pessimism with American innocence and moral complacency, and Southern identification with place and environment with American abstraction and disconnectness.[14]

Carter himself is aware of at least one of these regional characteristics, which he views as a "unique experience," that he would bring to the White House. He says, ". . . one of the strongest and best of these [experiences] is my relationship with poor people. That's where I came from. That's where I lived. Those are my people — not only whites, but particularly blacks — and it's not an accident that Andy Young [Representative Andrew Young] and Daddy King [the Rev. Martin Luther King Sr.] support me. They know that I understand their problems. They know that I've demonstrated an eagerness to solve them, and I think the strength of this country in the future is dependent on that. . . ."[15]

Carter has the Southerner's strong feeling of identity with place. He is part of the South's recent success story, but he also understands the region's past mood of pessimism and defeat. As he once said to a reporter, "It's hard for the country to understand, especially, the psyche or character of the Southerner; the kind of secret shame, the searching to redress old grievances."[16] Perhaps a Southerner who has been aware of these things all his life would be the best one to lead a country that has just begun to learn about failure and frustration.

Based on Carter's record as governor and his statements of policy during the campaign, it does look as if he would try to lead the country in a more positive direction than recent presidents have. He would be strong in the area of civil rights. He says that a beginning was made under Kennedy and Johnson, but that neither went far enough in terms of appointing blacks to policy-making positions in government. He would reorganize the federal bureaucracy, but would not cut back on spending for social programs. Here he believes that ". . . Johnson did an excellent job, but we still have a long way to go with national health care, reform of the welfare system, reform of the tax system. Those kinds of things would be my direct responsibility. . . ."[17] He would stress protection of the environment. In terms of foreign policy, the emphasis would be on human rights. In his major foreign policy address of the campaign, he said, "It is obviously un-American to interfere in the free political processes of another nation."[18] He would avoid secrecy in the conduct of foreign affairs and pursue a long-range policy based on respect for U.S. allies.

These are some very general things that could be expected from a Carter administration. His views on the presidency suggest that he would pursue these goals with the same determination he showed as governor of Georgia. He says that he believes that the country is best served by a president "who is strong and aggressive, innovative and sensitive, working with the Congress that's strong, independent, in harmony for a change, with mutual respect, for a change, in the open with a minimum of secrecy for a change."[19] But he adds that he doesn't believe that Congress is capable of leadership. "There's only one person in this nation that can speak with a clear voice for the American people. There's only one person who can set a standard of ethics and morality and excellence and greatness — or calling on the American people to make a sacrifice — and explain the purpose of the sacrifice — or answer difficult questions and proposing and carry out bold programs — or provide for a defense posture that will make us feel secure, a foreign policy that makes us proud once again — and that's the President."[20]

The above statement leaves little doubt that Carter as president would be the initiator of major policy rather than Congress. He would, for instance, present Congress with a tax reform package to vote on instead of waiting for it to draw up a bill. Given his views of the strong powers of the presidency, it's questionable how harmonious his relations with Congress would be. "Congress should fear him," commented one Georgian who observed Carter's rather harsh dealings with the state legislature. Carter himself predicts: ". . . It might be very contentious; it might be very competitive and it might even be combative — but I think the Congress is eager for some strong leadership, too, and I intend to be a strong leader. . . ."[21] The picture which emerges of a Carter presidency is one, which like his administration in Georgia, would be "highly controversial, aggressive, and combative."

Nevertheless, the prospect of a Carter presidency leaves open questions. We can't predict for certain what a man will do once in office; we can only speculate. And perhaps Carter himself isn't completely sure what kind of president he would be either, but he knows what he would like to be. With the possibility of becoming president before him, Jimmy Carter had this to say, ". . . While I don't fear the job, I certainly respect it and I know how much work it's going to take to do a good job. I would like to be a great President. . . ."[22]

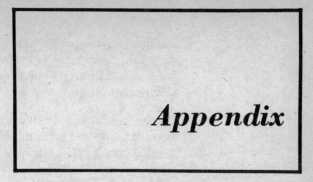

Appendix

A RUNDOWN ON THE CANDIDATE – JIMMY CARTER

Early Life

October 1, 1924   Jimmy Carter was born in southwest Georgia.

1943   Carter won an appointment at the U.S. Naval Academy in Annapolis.

1946   He was graduated from the U.S. Naval Academy.

He did 2 years of required surface duty.

1948   Carter applied for and received submarine duty. He served under Admiral Hyman Rickover on the development of the world's first atomic submarines. He also did graduate work in nuclear physics.

1953   He resigned his commission in the Navy when his father died, and returned to

Plains to run the family farm. He successfully built up his father's business by buying peanuts from individual farmers and
selling them to processors.

Carter made his first stand against
segregation by not joining the White Citizens' Council. His business was temporarily boycotted.

1961   Carter came under attack for his liberal
attitudes concerning black education
while a member and, later, chairman of
the Sumter County School Board.

His membership on the Sumter County
School Board gave him his first taste of
campaigning — and defeat — when he
pushed to consolidate the county and city
American school systems.

A Beginning in Politics

1962   **Election to the Senate**
Carter was elected to the Georgia Senate, where he spent 2 terms. This campaign gave him his first view of political
corruption.

Spring, 1966   **Democratic Nomination for Governor**
Carter lost the Democratic nomination
for Governor of Georgia. Maddox, who
won the nomination, was ultimately
elected Governor.

Democratic Contenders: Lt. Governor Byrd, Gray, Maddox, O'Kelley, Arnall, Carter.

Carter's Stand: He portrayed himself as a moderate. While he did not win this election, he achieved a great deal of popularity for an unknown candidate with only a limited time to campaign.

Carter's Campaign Issues: These were also used in later campaigns.

    1. People, not political bosses, should run the government.
    2. The government should be reorganized for efficiency, and fiscal prudence should be enacted.
    3. Honesty and openness should be the keynote of the government.

The Governorship

1966   Carter began working on a strategy for the gubernatorial campaign.

1967   Jimmy Carter became a "born again" Baptist.

1969   Carter had a poll done to determine voter attitudes.

1970   **The Gubernatorial Election:**
Carter vs. Suit. Carter won.

Democratic Contenders: Jenness,

Hargrett, Cox, Stoner, King, Sanders, Carter.

Carter's Stand: He took a conservative, antiestablishment stand to offset Sanders' liberal stand and gain all Wallace votes. His success has been attributed to his foresight in obtaining the conservative votes and to his intensive personal campaigning.

January 12, 1971
Jimmy Carter became Georgia's 76th Governor. See the complete text of his Inaugural Address on pages 196-200.

April 2, 1971
Carter proclaimed "American Fighting Men's Day" as a result of Calley's conviction in the My Lai Massacre.

1971
His record as governor through 1974:

Accomplishments:

1. A reorganizational and simplification of the government bureaucracy, using zero-based budgeting and improved investment policies. However, Carter's estimate of $50 million a year savings is a matter of dispute.

2. Judicial reform for the unification of the system, as well as an emphasis on the merit system in the selection of judges.

3. Improved health facilities for

mentally ill patients, drug addicts, alcoholics, etc.

4. Prison reform, with an emphasis toward rehabilitative programs.

5. An emphasis on pre-school, special, and vocational education. This proposal became a law.

6. Improved environmental protection, with controls for air and water pollution.

7. An improvement of race relations by prompting opportunities in education, jobs, and simple justice. He elected blacks to important positions. He also took a stand against forced busing.

8. "Government–in–sunshine" legislation and a campaign financial disclosure bill were passed.

9. Promoted economic growth by fostering trade relations with other countries.

Defeats and Problems:

1. Consumer protection.

2. A school drop-out rate still ranked among the highest in the country.

3. Overcrowded prisons.

4. Continued pollution.

5. A property tax bill, originally passed and then discontinued because it benefited corporations over individuals.

July 12, 1972   Carter nominated Scoop Jackson for president in the 1972 election.

Presidential Aspirations

1972   A 70-page game plan was prepared to help Carter win the 1976 presidential election:

1973   Carter was to be "projected as the heaviest of the governors in accomplishment."

1974   Carter was to be projected "as a leader in the Democratic Party and someone involved in bringing it back."

1975   Carter was to be projected as "a heavyweight thinker, leader in the party who had some ideas for running the country."

1976   Carter was to be projected as a presidential candidate for the Democratic party.

January 15, 1973   Carter proclaimed Martin Luther King, Jr., Day in Georgia. A year later he hung King's portrait in the state capitol building.

October 21, 1973   Carter, after the firing of Special Prosecutor Archibald Cox, went on national media to say that he thought Nixon was guilty and should resign.

1973 Carter volunteered to become the Democratic party's National Campaign Chairman for the 1974 elections to help reestablish a broad base for the Democratic party.

The Democratic party prepared a poll to delineate the most important issues among the American electorate. Many of their candidates won in the election.

Carter began planning his presidential campaign to be based on sincerity and trust rather than a discussion of specific issues.

December 12, 1974

Candidacy for the Democratic Presidential Nomination
Carter became a candidate for the Democratic presidential nomination. He gave the speech "For America's Third Century Why Not Our Best?" See pages 200-212 for the complete text.

January, 1975 Carter began a full-time campaign. Making a total effort all over the nation, he visited more than half the states. He was even aided by other candidates for a time, notably Scoop Jackson, who felt that Carter would help keep their supporters in line until their own campaigns were actively launched.

November, 1975	Carter impressed many at the National Democratic Issues Conference where he showed himself better informed than many of the old pro's.
Spring, 1976	Carter set out on a high-risk campaign strategy aimed at entering every presidential primary.
	Carter's Stand: Basically following a centrist approach with some deviations from right to left, Carter's overall position is designed to please the majority of the voters.
February 24, 1976	New Hampshire primary. Carter won with a plurality of the vote. The liberal vote was split 4 ways; Carter took the moderate vote.
March 9, 1976	Florida primary. Carter's first important victory over Wallace.
March 16, 1976	Illinois primary. Carter's second upset victory over Wallace.
April 6, 1976	Wisconsin primary. Carter won a narrow victory over liberal Udall in one of the most progressive states.
April 27, 1976	Pennsylvania primary. Carter won an important victory over Senator Henry Jackson. (Jackson then withdrew from the presidential race.)
May 18, 1976	Maryland primary. Carter lost to Brown.

May 18, 1976	Michigan primary. Carter barely defeated Udall.
June 8, 1976	Ohio primary. Carter won an important victory.
June 23, 1976	Carter delivered a major foreign policy address before The Foreign Policy Association in New York City.

JIMMY AND THE ISSUES

ISSUES	"CONSERVATIVE"	"MODERATE"	"LIBERAL"
Social			
Consumer Protection			✓
Crime		✓	
Education			✓
Health Care		✓	✓
Housing			✓
Labor		✓	
Social Security	✓	✓	
Welfare Reform	✓	✓	
Economics			
Anti-Trust Laws	✓		
Economy	✓	✓	
Revenue Sharing	✓		
Tax Reform		✓	
City/State/Federal Rights			
Attorney General and the Appointment of Federal Judges			✓
CIA		✓	

Issues	"Conservative"	"Moderate"	"Liberal"
Government and Bureaucracy	✓		
New York City	✓	✓	
Civil Rights			
Abortion	✓		
Amnesty		(Pardon) ✓	
Busing	✓	✓	
Women's Rights			✓
Agriculture		✓	
Defense and Military Spending		✓	
Energy	✓	✓	
Environment			✓
Foreign Affairs		✓	
Transportation		✓	✓
Urban Affairs		✓	

Note: The labels "conservative," "moderate," and "liberal" are provided solely for comparative purposes and are not meant to imply definitive party lines. An explanation of the candidate's views is provided in the following glossary. Where Jimmy Carter's stand on an issue does not fit into one "liberal" or "conservative" box, you will find that more than one box is checked.

Glossary

Although Jimmy Carter's presidential campaign is based more upon strong personal appeal than anything else, this does not mean that he lacks stands on the issues. In policy papers, interviews, and speeches he has spelled out his positions. He has been accused of vagueness, but when you get right down to it, he is probably no more elusive than the other candidates. While the stands he takes may seem confusing or even contradictory at times, this might be because complex problems often require complex answers.

Another problem with his stands on issues is that they don't all fit neatly into one "liberal" or "conservative" box. The fact is that on some issues his stand is moderate to conservative; on others, moderate to liberal. A look at the record also shows that some of his ideas have shifted in the past couple of years. But then he isn't the first politician to have changed his mind. In any event, here are his stands on the issues, as he has currently articulated them.

Abortion: Carter believes that abortion is wrong and that the government should try to discourage it by providing better sex education, family planning, and adoption procedures. However, he does not favor a constitutional amendment that would overturn the Supreme Court ruling permitting abortions.

Agriculture: Carter says that we need a "coherent, predictable and stable government policy" and a Secretary of Agriculture "who is inclined toward stability, predictability, and honest concern for the needs of family farmers and consumers." He also advocates that "We should again maintain a predictable, reasonably small and stable reserve of agricultural products. About a two months supply would be adequate with about one-half of these reserves being retained under the control of farmers to prevent government 'dumping' during times of moderate price increases."[1] He is in favor of continuing peanut subsidies, though on reduced levels, as well as of raising milk subsidies.

Amnesty: Carter would issue a "blanket pardon" for all Vietnam draft dodgers. He distinguishes between amnesty and pardon: "Amnesty says what you did was right. Pardon says whether what you did was right or wrong you are forgiven for it."

Antitrust Laws: Carter feels these laws must be rigidly enforced. Particularly concerned with the energy problem, Carter has emphasized restrictions on monopolies in the oil industry. He does not want companies to expand horizontally (i.e., own more than one major energy source), although he is not so opposed to companies expanding vertically since he feels that business can be hurt if some production processes are separated. Carter is adamant that interests remain separated between regulatory agencies and the regulated industries.

Attorney General and the Appointment of Federal Judges: Carter believes that the Attorney General should "be removed from politics," appointed for a specific period of time, and able to be removed from office only for misconduct as determined by both the President and "designated leaders of Congress." Carter believes that "All federal judges and prosecutors should be appointed strictly on the basis of merit without any consideration of political aspect or influence."[2]

Busing: Carter is not in favor of mandatory busing to achieve integration. He says that forced busing was tried in Atlanta but that it didn't work. "The only kids I have ever seen bused are poor children. I have never seen a rich child bused." Instead he prefers the voluntary plan adopted in Atlanta, whereby no child is bused against his or her will, but any child who wishes may be bused at the public expense. He also feels that black leadership should be adequately represented in the schools. However, if the federal courts rule in favor of mandatory busing, Carter would support their decision. He says "this is not the subject to be reopened with a constitutional amendment," and "I would really hate to see that done."[3]

CIA: Carter would not break up the Central Intelligence Agency (CIA) or restrict covert operations, but he would oversee the CIA to assure its involvement only in legal activities. "I will know what is going on, and if there is any wrongdoing, I will find out about it and I will see to it that those responsible are punished." He does not believe that the CIA should have been used in Angola.

Consumer Protection: Carter says that we need some

kind of national consumer education program. He also favors the creation of a strong federal consumer protection agency. "Such an agency could research information for all government hearings, presenting evidence supporting the voice of the consumer. Such an agency could assure all our citizens that their federal government is a government that speaks for them."[4] In addition, he would encourage consumer satisfaction through convenient small claims systems.

Crime: Carter thinks that the best way to reduce crime is to reduce unemployment. He favors registration of handguns, "a ban on the sale of cheap handguns, reasonable licensing provisions, including a waiting period and prohibition of ownership by anyone convicted of a crime involving a gun and by those not mentally competent." Nevertheless, he has not mentioned any registration for rifles and shotguns.

Carter feels that the death penalty should be retained for a few specific crimes, such as murder committed by a prisoner who is already serving a life sentence. The penalty must be imposed by a jury and reviewed in each case by a three-judge panel of the State Supreme Court. However, believing that drug laws are a little too rigid, he supports the decriminalization of possession of small amounts of marijuana.

Defense and Military Spending: Carter calls the Defense Department the "most wasteful agency in the Federal Government." He would cut its budget by 5%, but would not make cuts where he thought they could damage the country's national security. He opposes expensive weapons like the B-1 bomber, but favors constuction of the Trident, the Navy's new nuclear missile firing submarine. He says that "Our ultimate goal should be the reduction of nuclear weapons, in all nations, to zero," but admits that this probably would not occur during his lifetime.

Economy: Carter gives top priority to jobs. He believes that his administration would be able to get the unemployment rate down to below 5% without causing greater inflation "because our economy is presently performing so far below capacity." He would attack the problem of unemployment primarily through the private sector, with the federal government serving as the employer only as a last resort. He now supports the Humphrey-Hawkins full employment bill because he says the latest version of the bill leans toward his approach. He believes that through various subsidies and taxes, the federal government should stimulate the hiring of the unemployed, the young, and women in the private sector, and encourage employers to retain workers during cyclical downturns. Approximately 800,000 summer jobs would be provided for young people, and the scope of the Comprehensive Employment Training Program would be increased from 300,000 to 600,000 participants. Carter has expressed a commitment to revitalizing the cities, and would, if it seemed necessary, reinstate such Depression-era agencies as the Civilian Conservation Corps and the Works Progress Administration.

To curb inflation, he would increase the productivity of the economy, enforce consumer and anti-trust legislation as well as increase free-market competition, and shift from a tight-money policy to one that would encourage lower interest rates and make investment capital more available. Carter favors standby wage and price controls that he as President could apply selectively. He would preserve the independence of the Federal Reserve Board, but would want to appoint his own Federal Reserve Chairman.

Cautious on government spending, Carter calls for long-range economic planning through a system of three-year budgets. He has said that he would want to maintain a balanced national budget with full employment and to sustain a high level of economic growth while avoiding any reductions in funding for social programs. An advocate of our private enterprise system, Carter is not in favor of broad national planning by the government. He has said that he is against the "rigid, bureaucratic, centralized planning" of Communist countries.[5] Instead, he sees the need for "coordinated" government planning to deal with economic problems. His principal economic adviser is Professor Lawrence R. Klein of the Wharton School of Business, University of Pennsylvania.

Education: Carter, who feels that the federal government should pay a higher percentage of the cost of public education, gives early priority to the initiation of a comprehensive education program. His program would include such changes as the creation of a separate Department of Education, greater vocational and career opportunities, increased federal expenditures to provide for the education of the handicapped, reforms to strengthen colleges and universities in financially troubled times, and more educational opportunities for the elderly.

Energy: According to Carter, "The major thrust of the energy problem should be away from oil toward coal and solar energy. . . ."[6] He says that "It is unlikely that we will be totally independent of oil imports during this century," but that we should stress conservation. And only if conservation measures fail, should excise taxes be imposed on petroleum products. He would like domestic oil prices to be kept below those of O.P.E.C. oil although he says that any further oil embargo would be responded to as an "economic declaration of war." If necessary, he even feels that the Federal Energy Agency should ration oil to the states. (New natural gas prices would be regulated.) Anti-trust laws should be enforced, but Carter does not recommend the total vertical break-up of petroleum conglomerates. Rather, he says that oil companies should not be allowed to own other types of energy companies.

Carter feels that conservation must apply to more than oil, however. Unnecessary electrical power plants should not be built, rates should be structured to discourage consumption, and automobiles and electrical appliances should meet certain efficiency standards. The former Rickover disciple believes we should cut back drastically on our reliance to atomic power as a source of energy because of the dangers and the high costs involved. He calls for an agreement between the United States and the Soviet Union to halt all nuclear testing on a 5-year basis, and he advocates a ban on the exportation of small fuel reprocessing plants and bomb factories.

Environment: Carter supports land-use planning on a regional and national basis, feeling there is a need for national planned development in terms of urban and rural balance. He is against methods of producing more energy that will have an adverse effect on air and water quality.

Foreign Affairs: Carter says that "We must never again keep secret the evolution of our foreign policy from the Congress and the American people."[7] He is critical of Kissenger for his secrecy, and would definitely not keep him on as Secretary of State.

Carter supports the principle of detente with the Soviet Union, but feels that the U.S. has not benefited enough from it, and he supports expanded U.S.-Chinese trade relations. He feels we should avoid future "Vietnam's" (e.g., the Third World nations) and withdraw most American troops from the Philippines, Korea, and Thailand. He would also like U.S. military presence in Europe to be reduced, with the NATO countries taking on more responsibility for the defense of Western Europe. On the subject of the Panama Canal, Carter would retain "actual practical control" while yielding part of the "sovereignty" over the Canal Zone, and renegotiating U.S. payments to Panama.

"Our friends and allies" — Japan, Latin American, Western Europe, and Israel — should be our first priorities for support according to Carter, but the door shouldn't be closed on Communist leaders in Italy if they are successful. As for the situation in the Middle East, Carter says, "our nation's commitment is to the preservation of Israel, its right to exist in peace.". He feels that "The legitimate interests of the Palestinians have to be recognized," but would not recognize the PLO until they have convinced him that they recognize Israel's right to exist in peace. He would respond to a future Arab oil boycott with a declaration of economic war.

Carter's chief foreign policy adviser is Zbigniew Brzezinski, a professor at Columbia University, and a State Department official during the Johnson administration.

Government and Bureaucracy: Carter says, "Our government in Washington now is a horrible bureaucratic mess. It is disorganized, wasteful, has no purpose, and its policies — when they exist — are incomprehensible or devised by special interest groups with little regard for the welfare of the average American citizen."[8] The first legislation that he would send to Congress would begin a complete overhaul of the federal bureaucracy and budgeting systems. Zero-based budgeting that requires annual justification of all items in the budget, rather than just the new programs or the increases, will be required for all federal departments, bureaus, and boards. Next, Carter would reorganize the bureaucratic structure, reducing 1900 federal departments to no more than 200, "with great savings in tax money and a streamlining of services to the people."

Health Care: Carter says he favors a nationwide, comprehensive mandatory health insurance program. His plan is that such a program would be financed through both the employer and the payroll taxes, as well as general revenue taxes. Patients would still be free to choose their own physician, but the federal government would set doctor's fees and establish controls to monitor the cost and quality of health care. Carter's proposal is very similar to the Kennedy-Corman health security bill now before Congress. Interested in promoting preventive medicine, Carter would also like to have more supportive personnel, as paraprofessionals and nurse practitioners, available to patients.

Housing: Carter believes that "A direct subsidy of new housing units is essential in order to construct new low- and middle-income housing and to stimulate the construction industry. We should work toward providing low-income citizens with an adequate housing allowance. . . . The Federal Government can establish criteria for allocating housing funds, [etc.]. . . . But we must let local authorities . . . maintain low-income housing."[9] He feels that realtors should play a greater part in land-use planning and that there should be a steady supply of credit to reduce boom and bust cycles in the housing industry. In addition, he feels that it is necessary to focus on the restoration and conservation of existing neighborhoods as well as the creation of new ones.

Labor: Carter says that he would sign the repeal of the Taft-Hartley right-to-work law which forbids closed shops, but would not promote a repeal movement. He also says he believes in collective bargaining for all employees and favors arbitration for public service employees. He advocates minimum wage laws.

New York City: Carter believes that providing New York City with a limited loan during its financial crisis set a bad precedent, and encouraged urban financial irresponsibility. He would have acted to insure the city's "fiscal integrity" only after both the city and state had taken steps to guarantee a balanced budget. However, his administration would consider the creation of a Federal Municipalities Securities Corporation to help cities market their bonds at lower interest rates.

Revenue Sharing: Funds should go directly to local cities and communities rather than to the states. (This represents a change from his previous position where, as governor; he advocated that funds should go directly to the states.)

Social Security: Carter feels this system will be sound in the years to come. However, to assure that more money flows in than out, he advocates keeping inflation and unemployment down, as well as levying taxes on incomes ranging from $3,600 to $20-22,000 rather than from $2,760 to $15,300. He feels this salary range is more equitable, for it taxes those better able to afford it. Interested in keeping Social Security purely a retirement system, he advocates its separation from other federal systems.

Tax Reform: Carter says that our national tax system is a "disgrace," He advocates tax reform "not to soak the rich but as a program that would soak the people who don't pay their fair share of taxes. I think many wealthy persons pay their fair shares. I'm a wealthy man myself. But I want a simple equitable tax system that would shift the tax burden away from low- and middle-income groups."[10]

The simplified more progressive tax rate system Carter envisions would eliminate most deductions (including those on home mortgage payments) and would treat all personal income the same. It would modify corporate taxes to discourage corporations from moving their operations to other countries. A detailed comprehensive program of tax reform would not be forthcoming until he would be in office for at least a year.

Transportation: Carter calls for greater federal involvement in the country's transportation system, particularly regarding coordination of the various modes of mass transportation. He would use the Highway Trust Fund to maintain the present highway system rather than build new highways, and to improve mass transportation in urban areas. He supports the idea of a total transportation fund, which would do away with the current preference given to highways. Carter thinks that our railroads should receive more attention because of the savings they offer in terms of fuel, operating, and pollution costs. In addition, he would end much of the regulation of the trucking industry. Carter feels that the Concorde should not be allowed to land in the U.S. because of the environmental dangers involved.

Urban Affairs: Aware that cities are losing many of their affluent citizens and businesses, Carter has provided programs designed to meet the major problem areas of unemployment, urban decay, a declining tax base, crime, and a lack of parks and open spaces. To meet individual needs, he has proposed employment incentives for private employers and a federal public needs program, as well as welfare reform. To meet urban fiscal needs, he has proposed aid in creating new jobs and in maintaining current service levels, an extension of revenue sharing (so that it may be used for health and social services), and an assist in marketing bonds and in reducing interest levels. He will also provide federal subsidy and low-interest loans to encourage low- and middle-class housing, additional funds for public transportation, a simpler judicial system with regulation of handguns and prisoner rehabilitation, an emphasis on parks, and improved communication with city mayors.

Welfare Reform: Carter feels that 1.3 million of the current welfare recipients are able to work, and that they should be taken off welfare and given either training or a job. For the remaining 90% there should be a fairly uniform payment — one basic payment, thereby eliminating food stamps — with a built-in work incentive for those who can hold part-time jobs. This payment should come from state and federal revenues so that local areas are relieved of the responsibility. He advocates having one or two basic programs rather than a hundred so that welfare workers "work with people rather than paper."

Women's Rights: Carter supports the Equal Rights Amendment. When he was governor, he worked to open more government positions to women. He says, "I am firmly committed to equality between women and men and in promoting a partnership concept in all aspects of life." As president, he would see to it that "laws prohibiting sex discrimination in employment, advancement, education, training, credit and housing be strictly enforced;" "strong efforts be made to create federal legislation and guidelines to eliminate sex discrimination in health and disability insurance plans;" "social security laws be revised so that women would no longer be penalized;" "women have equal access to health care systems and voluntary family planning programs;" "adequate childcare be made available to all parents who need such care for their children;" and "strong efforts be made to reform existing rape laws."[11] Carter supports the passage of the National Rape Prevention and Control Act. In addition, he advocates flexible hours for full-time employees.

KEYNOTE SPEECHES

★ ★ ★

Inaugural Address
[Gubernatorial]

January 12, 1971

Governor Maddox and other fellow Georgians:

It is a long way from Plains to Atlanta. I started the trip four and a half years ago and, with a four year detour, I finally made it. I thank you all for making it possible for me to be here on what is certainly the greatest day of my life. But now the election is over, and I realize that the test of a man is not how well he campaigned, but how effectively he meets the challenges and responsibilities of the office.

I shall only take a few minutes today to summarize my feelings about Georgia. Later this week my program will be described in some detail in my State of the State and Budget messages to the House and Senate.

I am grateful and proud to have with us the Naval Academy Band, because it reminds me as it did when I was a midshipman of the love of our Nation and of its goals and ideals. Our Country was founded on the premise that government continually derives its power from independent and free men. If it is to survive, confident and courageous citizens must be willing to assume responsibility for the quality of our government at any particular time in history.

This is a time for truth and frankness. The next four years will not be easy ones. The problems we face will not solve themselves. They demand from us the utmost in dedication and unselfishness from each of us. But this is also a time for greatness. Our people are determined to overcome the handicaps of the past and to meet the opportunities of the future with confidence and with courage.

Our people are our most precious possession and we cannot afford to waste the talents and abilities given by God to one single Georgian. Every adult illiterate, every school dropout, every untrained retarded child is an indictment of us all. Our state pays a terrible and continuing human financial price for these failures. It is time to end this waste. If Switzerland and Israel and other people can eliminate illiteracy, then so can we. The responsibility is our own, and as Governor, I will not shirk this responsibility.

At the end of a long campaign, I believe I know our people as well as anyone. Based on this knowledge of Georgians North and South, Rural and Urban, liberal and conservative, I say to you quite frankly that the time for racial discrimination is over. Our people have already made this major and difficult decision, but we cannot underestimate the challenge of hundreds of minor decisions yet to be made. Our inherent human charity and our religious beliefs will be taxed to the limit. No poor, rural, weak, or black person should ever have to bear the additional burden of being deprived of the opportunity of an education, a job or simple justice. We Georgians are fully capable of making our judgments and managing our own affairs. We who are strong or in positions of leadership must realize that the responsibility for making correct decisions in the future is ours. As Governor, I will never shirk this responsibility.

Georgia is a state of great natural beauty and promise, but the quality of our natural surroundings is threatened because of avarice, selfishness, procrastination and neglect. Change and development are necessary for the growth of our population and for the progress of our agricultural, recreational, and industrial life. Our challenge is to insure that such activities avoid destruction and dereliction of our environment. The responsibility for meeting this challenge is our own. As Governor, I will not shirk this responsibility.

In Georgia, we are determined that the law shall be enforced. Peace officers must have our appreciation and complete support. We cannot educate a child, build a highway, equalize tax burdens, create harmony among our people, or preserve basic human freedom unless we have an orderly society. Crime and lack of justice are especially cruel to those who are least able to protect themselves. Swift arrest and trial and fair punishment should be expected by those who would break our laws. It is equally important to us that every effort be made to rehabilitate law breakers into useful and productive members of society. We have not yet attained these goals in Georgia, but now we must. The proper function of a government is to make it easy for man to do good and difficult for him to do evil. This responsibility is our own. I will not shirk this responsibility.

Like thousands of other businessmen in Georgia, I have always attempted to conduct my business in an honest and efficient manner. Like thousands of other citizens, I expect no less of government.

The function of government should be administered so as to justify confidence and pride.

Taxes should be minimal and fair.

Rural and urban people should easily discern the mutuality of their goals and opportunities.

We should make our major investments in people, not buildings.

With wisdom and judgment we should take future actions according to carefully considered long-range plans and priorities.

Governments closest to the people should be strengthened, and the efforts of our local, state and national governments need to be thoroughly coordinated.

We should remember that our state can best be served by a strong and independent governor, working with a strong and independent legislature.

Government is a contrivance of human wisdom to provide for human wants. Men have a right to expect that these wants will be provided by this wisdom.

The test of a government is not how popular it is with the powerful and privileged few, but how honestly and fairly it deals with the many who must depend upon it.

William Jennings Bryan said, "Destiny is not a matter of chance, it is a matter of choice. Destiny is not a thing to be waited for, it is a thing to be achieved."

Here around me are seated the members of the Georgia Legislature and other State Officials. They are dedicated and honest men and women. They love this state as you love it. But no group of elected officers, no matter how dedicated or enlightened, can control the destiny of a great state like ours. What officials can solve alone the problems of crime, welfare, illiteracy, disease, injustice, pollution, and waste? This control rests in *your* hands, the people of Georgia.

In a democracy, no government can be stronger, or wiser, or more just than its people. The idealism of the college student, the compassion of a woman, the common sense of the businessman, the time and experience of a retired couple, and the vision of political leaders must all be harnessed to bring out the best in our State.

As I have said many times during the last few years,

I am determined that at the end of this administration we shall be able to stand up anywhere in the world — in New York, California, or Florida and say "I'm a Georgian" — and be proud of it.

I welcome the challenge and the opportunity of serving as Governor of our State during the next four years. I promise you my best. I ask for your best.

★ ★ ★

For America's Third Century Why Not Our Best?

STANDARDS OF EXCELLENCE

[Speech Announcing Candidacy for the Democratic Presidential Nomination]

By JIMMY CARTER, *Governor of Georgia*

Delivered before the National Press Club, Washington, D.C., December 12, 1974

We Americans are a great and diverse people. We take full advantage of our rights to develop wideranging interests and responsibilities. For instance, I am a farmer, an engineer, a businessman, a planner, a scientist, a governor and a Christian. Each of you is an individual and different from all the others.

Yet we Americans have shared one thing in common: a belief in the greatness of our Country.

We have dared to dream great dreams for our Nation. We have taken quite literally the promises of decency, equality, and freedom — of an honest and responsible government.

What has now become of these great dreams?

— That all Americans stand equal before the law;

— That we enjoy a right to pursue health, happiness and prosperity in privacy and safety;

— That government be controlled by its citizens and not the other way around;

— That this Country set a standard within the community of nations of courage, compassion, integrity, and dedication to basic human rights and freedoms.

Our commitments to these dreams has been sapped by debilitating compromise, acceptance of mediocrity, subservience to special interests, and an absence of executive vision and direction.

Having worked during the last twenty years in local, state and national affairs, I have learned a great deal about our people.

I tell you that their great dreams still live within the collective heart of this Nation.

Recently we have discovered that our trust has been betrayed. The veils of secrecy have seemed to thicken around Washington. The purposes and goals of our country are uncertain and sometimes even suspect.

Our people are understandably concerned about this lack of competence and integrity. The root of the problem is not so much that our people have lost confidence in government, but that government has demonstrated time and again its lack of confidence in the people.

Our political leaders have simply underestimated the innate quality of our people.

With the shame of Watergate still with us and our 200th birthday just ahead, it is time for us to reaffirm and to strengthen our ethical and spiritual and political beliefs.

There must be no lowering of these standards, no acceptance of mediocrity in any aspect of our private or public lives.

In our homes, or at worship we are ever reminded of what we ought to do and what we ought to be. Our government can and must represent the best and the highest ideals of those of us who voluntarily submit to its authority.

Politicians who seek to further their political careers through appeals to our doubts, fears and prejudices will be exposed and rejected.

For too long political leaders have been isolated from the people. They have made decisions from an ivory tower. Few have ever seen personally the direct impact of government programs involving welfare, prisons, mental institutions, unemployment, school busing or public housing. Our people feel that they have little access to the core of government and little influence with elected officials.

Now it is time for this chasm between people and government to be bridged, and for American citizens to join in shaping our Nation's future.

Now is the time for new leadership and new ideas to make a reality of these dreams, still held by our people.

To begin with, the confidence of people in our own government must be restored. But too many officials do not deserve that confidence.

There is a simple and effective way for public officials to regain public trust — be trustworthy!

But there are also specific steps that must be taken.

We need an all-inclusive sunshine law in Washington so that special interests will not retain their exclusive access behind closed doors. Except in a few rare cases, there is no reason for secret meetings of regulatory agencies, other executive departments or congressional committees. Such meetings must be opened to the public, all votes recorded, and complete news media coverage authorized and encouraged.

Absolutely no gifts of value should ever again be permitted to a public official.

Complete revelation of all business and financial involvements of major officials should be required, and none should be continued which constitute a possible conflict with the public interest.

Regulatory agencies must not be managed by representatives of the industry being regulated, and no personnel transfers between agency and the industry should be made within a period of four full years.

Public financing of campaigns should be extended to members of Congress.

The activities of lobbyists must be more thoroughly revealed and controlled.

Minimum secrecy within government should be matched with maximum personal privacy for private citizens.

All federal judges, diplomats and other major officals should be selected on a strict basis of merit. For many years in the State Department we have chosen from among almost 16,000 applicants about 110 of our Nation's finest young leaders to represent us in the international world. But we top this off with the disgraceful and counterproductive policy of appointing unqualified persons to major diplomatic posts as political payoffs. This must be stopped immediately. Every effort should be extended to encourage full participation by our people in their own governments' processes, including universal voter registration for elections.

We must insure better public understanding of executive policy, and better exchange of ideas between the Congress and the White House. To do this, Cabinet members representing the President should meet in scheduled public interrogation sessions with the full bodies of Congress.

All our citizens must know that they will be treated fairly. To quote from my own inauguration speech of four years ago: "The time for racial discrimination is over. Our people have already made this major and difficult decision, but we cannot underestimate the challenge of hundreds of minor decisions yet to be made. No poor, rural, weak or black person should ever have to bear the additional burden of being deprived of the opportunity of an education, a job or simple justice."

We must meet this firm national commitment without equivocation or timidity in every aspect of private and public life.

As important as honesty and openness are — they are not enough. There must be substance and logical direction in government.

The mechanism of our government should be understandable, efficient and economical . . . and it can be.

We must give top priority to a drastic and thorough revision of the federal bureaucracy, to its budgeting system and to the procedures for analyzing the effectiveness of its many varied services. Tight businesslike management and planning techniques must be instituted and maintained, utilizing the full authority and personal involvement of the President himself.

This is no job for the fainthearted. It will be met with violent opposition from those who now enjoy a special privilege, those who prefer to work in the dark, or those whose private fiefdoms are threatened.

In Georgia, we met that opposition head on — and we won!

We abolished 278 of our 300 agencies.

We evolved clearly defined goals and policies in every part of government.

We developed and implemented a remarkably effective system of zero base budgeting.

We instituted tough performance auditing to insure proper conduct and efficient delivery of services.

Steps like these can insure a full return on our hard-earned tax dollars. These procedures are working in state capitols around the Nation and in successful businesses, both large and small.

They can and they will work in Washington.

Our Nation now has no understandable national purpose, no clearly defined goals, and no organizational mechanism to develop or achieve such purposes or goals. We move from one crisis to the next as if they were fads, even though the previous one hasn't been solved.

The Bible says: "If the trumpet give an uncertain sound, who shall prepare himself to the battle." As a planner and a businessman, and a chief executive, I know from experience that uncertainty is also a devastating affliction in private life and in government. Coordination of different programs is impossible. There is no clear vision of what is to be accomplished, everyone struggles for temporary advantage, and there is no way to monitor how effectively services are delivered.

What is our national policy for the production, acquisition, distribution or consumption of energy in times of shortage or doubtful supply?

There is no policy!

What are our long-range goals in health care, transportation, land use, economic development, waste disposal or housing?

There are no goals!

The tremendous resources of our people and of our chosen leaders can be harnessed to devise effective, understandable and practical goals and policies in every realm of public life.

A government that is honest and competent, with clear purpose and strong leadership can work with the American people to meet the challenges of the present and the future.

We can then face together the tough long-range solutions to our economic woes. Our people are ready to make personal sacrifices when clear national economic policies are devised and understood.

We are grossly wasting our energy resources and other precious raw materials as though their supply was infinite. We must even face the prospect of changing our basic ways of living. This change will either be made on our own initiative in a planned and rational way, or forced on us with chaos and suffering by the inexorable laws of nature.

Energy imports and consumption must be reduced, free competition enhanced by rigid enforcement of antitrust laws, and general monetary growth restrained. Pinpointed federal programs can ease the more acute pains of recession, such as now exist in the construction industry. We should consider extension of unemployment compensation, the stimulation of investments, public subsidizing of employment, and surtaxes on excess profits.

We are still floundering and equivocating about protection of our environment. Neither designers of automobiles, mayors of cities, power companies, farmers, nor those of us who simply have to breathe the air, love beauty, and would like to fish or swim in pure water have the slightest idea in God's world what is coming out of Washington next! What does come next must be a firm commitment to pure air, clean water and unspoiled land.

Almost twenty years after its conception we have not finished the basic interstate highway system. To many lobbyists who haunt the capitol buildings of the Nation, ground transportation still means only more highways and more automobiles — the bigger, the better. We must have a national commitment to transportation capabilities which will encourage the most efficient movement of American people and cargo.

Gross tax inequities are being perpetuated. The most surely taxed income is that which is derived from the sweat of manual labor. Carefully contrived loopholes let the total tax burden shift more and more toward the average wage earner. The largest corporations pay the lowest tax rates and some with very high profits pay no tax at all.

When a business executive can charge off a $50 luncheon on a tax return and a truck driver cannot deduct his $1.50 sandwich — when oil companies pay less than 5% on their earnings while employees of the company pay at least three times this rate — when many pay no taxes on incomes of more than $100,000 — then we need basic tax reform!

Every American has a right to expect that laws will be administered in an evenhanded manner, but it seems that something is wrong even with our system of justice. Defendants who are repeatedly out on bail commit more crimes. Aggravating trial delays and endless litigation are common.

Citizens without influence often bear the brunt of prosecution while violators of antitrust laws and other white collar criminals are ignored and go unpunished.

Following recent presidential elections, our U.S. Attorney General has replaced the Postmaster General as the chief political appointee; and we have recently witnessed the prostitution of this most important law enforcement office. Special prosecutors had to be appointed simply to insure enforcement of the law! The Attorney General should be removed from politics.

The vast bureaucracy of government often fails to deliver needed social services to our people. High ideals and good intentions are not matched with rational, businesslike administration. The predictable result is frustration and discouragement among dedicated employees, recipients of services, and the American taxpayers.

There are about 25 million Americans who are classified as poor, two-thirds of whom happen to be white and half of whom receive welfare benefits. At least 10 percent of these are able to work. A massive bureaucracy of 2 million employees at all levels of government is attempting to administer more than 100 different programs of bewildering complexity. Case workers shuffle papers in a morass of red tape. Often it is financially profitable not to work and even to have a family disrupted by forcing the father to leave home. Some combined welfare payments exceed the average working family's income, while other needy families have difficulty obtaining a bare subsistence.

The word "welfare" no longer signifies how much we care, but often arouses feelings of contempt and even hatred.

Is a simplified, fair and compassionate welfare program beyond the capacity of our American government? I think not.

The quality of health care in this Nation depends

largely on economic status. It is often unavailable or costs too much. There is little commonality of effort between private and public health agencies or between physicians and other trained medical personnel. I expect the next Congress to pass a national health insurance law. But present government interest seems to be in merely shifting the costs of existing services to the federal taxpayer or to the employers. There is little interest in preventing the cripplers and killers of our people and providing improved health care for those who still need it most.

Is a practical and comprehensive national health program beyond the capacity of our American government? I think not.

Federal education laws must be simplified to substitute education for paper-shuffling grantsmanship. Local systems need federal funds to supplement their programs for students where wealth and tax base are inadequate.

Is a comprehensive education program beyond the capacity of the American people? I think not.

As a farmer, I have been appalled at the maladministration of our Nation's agricultural economy. We have seen the elimination of our valuable food reserves, which has contributed to wide fluctuations in commodity prices and wiped out dependable trade and export capabilities. Grain speculators and monopolistic processors have profited, while farmers are going bankrupt trying to produce food that consumers are going broke trying to buy.

I know this Nation can develop an agricultural policy which will insure a fair profit to our farmers and a fair price to consumers.

It is obvious that domestic and foreign affairs are directly interrelated. A necessary base for effective implementation of any foreign policy is to get our domestic house in order.

Coordination of effort among the leaders of our Nation should be established so that our farm production, industrial development, foreign trade, defense, energy and diplomatic policies are mutually supportive and not in conflict.

The time for American intervention in all the problems of the world is over. But we cannot retreat into isolationism. Ties of friendship and cooperation with our friends and neighbors must be strengthened. Our common interests must be understood and pursued. The integrity of Israel must be preserved. Highly personalized and narrowly focused diplomatic efforts, although sometimes successful, should be balanced with a more wide-ranging implementation of foreign policy by competent foreign service officers.

Our Nation's security is obviously of paramount importance, and everything must be done to insure adequate military preparedness. But there is no reason why our national defense establishment cannot also be efficient.

Waste and inefficiency are both costly to taxpayers and a danger to our own national existence. Strict management and budgetary control over the Pentagon should reduce the ratio of officers to men and of support forces to combat troops. I see no reason why the Chief of Naval Operations needs more Navy captains on his staff than we have serving on ships!

Misdirected efforts such as the construction of unnecessary porkbarrel projects by the Corps of Engineers must be terminated.

The biggest waste and danger of all is the unnecessary proliferation of atomic weapons throughout the world. Our ultimate goal should be the elimination of nuclear weapon capability among all nations. In the meantime, simple, careful and firm proposals to implement this mutual arms reduction should be pursued as a prime national purpose in all our negotiations with nuclear powers — present or potential.

Is the achievement of these and other goals beyond the capacity of our American government? I think not.

Our people are hungry for integrity and competence in government. In this confused and fast-changing, technological world we still have within us the capability for national greatness.

About three months ago I met with the governors of the other twelve original states in Philadelphia. Exactly 200 years after the convening of the First Continental Congress we walked down the same streets, then turned left and entered a small building named Carpenter's Hall. There we heard exactly the same prayer and sat in the same chairs occupied in September of 1774 by Samuel Adams, John Jay, John Adams, Patrick Henry, George Washington, and about forty-five other strong and opinionated leaders.

They held widely divergent views and they debated for weeks. They and others who joined them for the Second Continental Congress avoided the production of timid compromise resolutions. They were somehow inspired, and they reached for greatness. Their written premises formed the basis on which our Nation was begun.

I don't know whose chair I occupied, but sitting there I thought soberly about their times and ours. Their people were also discouraged, disillusioned and confused. But these early leaders acted with purpose and conviction.

I wondered to myself: Were they more competent, more intelligent or better educated than we? Were they more courageous? Did they have more compassion or love for their neighbors? Did they have deeper religious convictions? Were they more concerned about the future of their children than we?

I think not.

We are equally capable of correcting our faults, overcoming difficulties, managing our own affairs and facing the future with justifiable confidence.

I am convinced that among us 200 million Americans there is a willingness — even eagerness — to restore in our Country what has been lost — *if* we have understandable purposes and goals and a modicum of bold and inspired leadership.

Our government can express the highest common ideals of human beings — *if* we demand of its standards of excellence.

It is now time to stop and to ask ourselves the question which my last commanding officer, Admiral Hyman Rickover, asked me and every other young naval officer who serves, or has served in an atomic submarine.

For our Nation — for all of us — that question is, "Why not the best?"

JIMMY AND THE PRESS

Why I Support Jimmy Carter

REP. ANDREW YOUNG

Blacks have always known that our best allies are those Southern whites who have dared to live by their religious principles and who have been through the fire of persecution because of it. Northern liberals don't know how many such courageous souls there are. Only those who leave, either by choice or force, come to national attention. Tom Wicker, Chuck Morgan of ACLU, Bill Moyers and Willie Morris are widely recognized because they left, but there are many more who stayed and worked very effectively to deal with the problems of race and economic deprivation in our region.

Jimmy Carter left the South to complete his education and see the world in a Navy submarine, but he came back just as the turmoil of racial change erupted. A stubborn, independent spirit and a deep compassion enabled him to survive the moral contradictions exploding around him. He learned to love from his mother, one of the truly great women of our time. Southern women, whether black or white, have always been more free than the men.

The South has always been able to tolerate a few whites who were eccentric in their private lives and beliefs. It was only as you sought publicly to demon-

Andrew Young is a Democratic member of Congress from Georgia.
Reprinted by permission of *The Nation* © 1976. 3 April, 1976.

strate your convictions that attacks came from white citizens.

Before he entered politics, Carter refused membership in the White Citizens' Council. In his first elected office, he blocked the transfer of public school funds to segregated academies in Sumter County. His peanut warehouse suffered a brief boycott, but generally, he lived an independent, principled life through the 1950s and early 1960s. Jimmy's credentials are certainly as valid as a liberal voting record in the safety of the United States Congress.

I'm a romantic and an idealist, so it was very difficult for me to ignore such a moral and political success story. Admittedly, these alone do not qualify a man to be President of the United States. They do qualify him as a representative of the New South and a voice capable of ending the Wallace myth, which led politicians of both parties to turn to the Right. The principles of tolerance and fairness led me into a relationship with Jimmy Carter, but it is hard political reality that keeps me there.

In the primaries of recent weeks, first Florida, then Illinois and North Carolina ended up as battlegrounds with George Wallace. Only Jimmy Carter dared take him on in the conservative Florida panhandle. In 1972 Florida was the burying ground for progressive candidates, and a mood was set which Nixon exploited and which has dominated the nation for the past four years. Defeating Wallace in Florida had to be the number-one priority of any liberal strategy. The domestic agenda would be determined by the outcome.

Meanwhile, the Massachusetts primary had brought forth a new reality. Sen. Henry Jackson, exploiting the busing issue and the Moynihan "get tough" policy at the

JIM CARTER

United Nations, and supported by the conservative wing of the AFL-CIO, put together a surprise victory there. The result was: *(1)* the demise of Birch Bayh, the liberal who had the best chance of beating Jackson in New York; *(2)* the resurgence of cold-war foreign policy and a dangerous swing to the Right internationally; *(3)* the potential of a Jackson boom sweeping the big industrial states and creating a very negative national mood in both domestic and foreign policy; and *(4)* the possibility of a "private" deal with Wallace that would give Jackson the nomination and Wallace the influence behind the scenes, though not a place on the ticket. Jimmy Carter has the best chance to minimize Jackson's support in New York City, and his upstate and Long Island organizations might balance out the results on April 6.

In any event, the role of supporters is to provide insights and access to the voters, but the candidate himself must win the votes. Jimmy Carter has found one key to the American mood. He has put together a well-organized and efficient campaign. He has demonstrated a capacity to reach a broad segment of the Democratic electorate and especially black voters who make up more than 20 per cent of any national Democratic vote.

Carter grew up with black folk. Plains, Ga., has 300 white and 400 black citizens. He governed in a state with a 29 per cent black voting population. Fully one-third of the black professionals across the nation studied in the six institutions of higher education in Atlanta. Carter is a product of the Southern church and knows the language and culture of the black community. There are still more voting blacks in churches than in labor unions or political organizations. Jimmy Carter probably has more black staff than all the other candidates put together — not just organizing the black vote but keeping financial records and reporting to the Federal Elections Commission.

Any Democratic President must be able to reach black voters while not alienating middle America. Jimmy has done this quite successfully in Florida, Massachusetts and Illinois. He is perhaps the most electable of the Democrats in a race against Gerald Ford. There is a yearning for something different, as James Reston has pointed out, and as ninety-one new Congresspersons demonstrate. We must have a Democratic President in 1976. The nation could hardly survive four more years of Republican mismanagement and economic disaster. The difference between the Democratic candidates, except for Wallace, will be a matter of emphasis — quite an important difference, but not nearly as great as the gap between the parties.

Regardless of party, however, any President must cope with a Congress that is determined to share governmental power. There will be no more imperial Presidency. An overwhelmingly Democratic legislature will set the national program in the 95th Congress. We are not searching for ideas and programs; we are looking for effective administration and leadership from the executive branch. Full employment, national health insurance, tax reform and urban redevelopment will be the agenda for any Democrat in the White House.

Will Carter make a good President? Martin Luther King, Jr. was fond of quoting: "Greatness is characterized by antitheses strongly marked. A great man must be one with a tough mind and a tender heart." Jimmy Carter is such a man. He reads constantly, he listens and seeks advice from a variety of sources, then makes up his own mind. Once he's made up his mind, he's as tough as the proverbial Georgia Bulldog, though he went to Georgia Tech and the Naval Academy.

I remember flying in a helicopter down Georgia's Chattahoochee River with Jimmy Carter and Scoop Jackson and listening to Jimmy, who was Governor then, discuss environmental issues with Scoop. He not only held his own but took Scoop on in energy questions as well. Jimmy is like that. He sized up all the Presidential prospects who came through Georgia while he was Governor, and decided they didn't know any more than he did and that he could outwork any of them. So why not run for President? The early primaries have proved that he may have been right.

As Governor he did not shrink from challenges. He tried to anticipate them and head off crises. He brought in consultants from M.I.T. to help with governmental reorganization, and hired a young prison reformer from Connecticut to do something about Georgia's archaic prisons (the system was so bad it gave the newcomer a heart attack in six months). Carter was the first Georgia Governor to show publicly his respect for blacks and organized labor in state politics. Prior to his administration, the state's conservative mood viewed open contacts with labor and blacks as fatal to a politician's career in Georgia. Carter addressed the state AFL-CIO annual dinner and worked to end the "waiting week," which was required before workers could receive unemployment compensation.

Perhaps the most significant thing he did was to deputize every high school principal in the state as a voting registrar. This meant that registration was easy and accessible in all of Georgia's 159 counties for blacks and whites alike. (By contrast, Lyndon Johnson sent federal voting referees to only 106 Southern counties, most of them in Alabama and Mississippi. Nixon never used federal power to protect minority voting rights.)

The new participation in Georgia politics owes a lot to Jimmy's executive initiative. He was so successful that he almost lost out as a delegate to the 1972 convention. A black college student came within fifteen votes of beating him.

The toughest battles of his administration were on environmental issues. If you judge by the behavior of Georgia's Congressional delegation or state legislature, you might decide there is little or no political gain to be found in fighting to protect the environment. Yet Jimmy confronted the Corps of Engineers, the real estate lobby and the highway and construction lobbies which have dominated Georgia politics for half a century. He mobilized enough citizen support to win on several key environmental issues in the state. Whenever there was a choice of avoiding a challenge, compromising an issue or battling head-on, he invariably chose to fight. That attitude does much to explain both his success and his many enemies in Georgia. Carter is a stranger to liberal rhetoric and ideology. He is an engineer and farmer. He may even deny the liberal formulas which come from Ivy League colleges and liberal arts education. But his heart is right, his instincts are sound and his training is very practical. He is not much on analysis of problems and debate on issues, but he does solve problems. He defies labeling. His appeal is intensely personal, not ideological. He starts with the problems of people and works to discover effective and efficient solutions.

There will be a lot of close scrutiny of Jimmy Carter. He asks for it and seems to have built a campaign on the question of character. Cynics are both intrigued and offended by this. My bet is that he'll come through; perhaps a bit bruised and scarred by it all, but nevertheless unbowed.

Why I Don't Support Jimmy Carter

JULIAN BOND

The democratic process that elects the President of the United States is essentially an elimination contest in which voters are presented with a series of diminishing options. The voter's first choice of December isn't available by March, and the March contender who tickles the public fancy may have wilted by June. As they search for a candidate whose political views and voting record are closest to their own, they remain loyal to certain political principles. And that's why I support Rep. Morris Udall of Arizona. That's why I can't support Jimmy Carter of Georgia.

As a veteran of the 1968 McCarthy campaign, and the 1972 McGovern campaign, I've tried to seek and support candidates whose accomplishments and current statements demonstrate their support of traditionally liberal principles and humanistic values in which I believe. Morris Udall supports those principles and values. Jimmy Carter does not.

Representative Udall's fourteen-year record in the Congress places him squarely in the liberal column, and demonstrates that his commitment to social justice didn't begin with his ambition to become President. Jimmy Carter nominated "Scoop" Jackson for President in Miami in 1972, then attempted to organize a "stop-McGovern" movement. When that failed, he approached at least two black Georgia delegates and asked us to mention his name to McGovern as a possible running mate. I did so twice, both before and after Eagleton, but now Carter lies and says it wasn't so.

Julian Bond is a Democratic member of the Georgia Senate.
Reprinted by permission of *The Nation* © 1976. 17 April, 1976.

As a candidate for governor of Georgia, Carter courted the Wallace vote, and said nice things about Lester Maddox. Ray Abernathy, who worked for Carter's advertising agency during the gubernatorial campaign, says he used Carter campaign funds to pay for the media advertising of a black candidate for governor, who would pull votes away from Carter's liberal opponent, former Gov. Carl Sanders. Carter let Georgia's white voters know he could win "without a single black vote." He won the primary with less than 10 per cent of that vote.

At the June 1972 Democratic Governors' Conference in Omaha, Carter introduced resolutions asking that

Margulies - Rothco Cartoons

the war in Vietnam *not* be an issue in the 1972 campaign; praising J. Edgar Hoover for his "service" to the nation, and urging both Gov. George Wallace of Alabama and Gov. John Bell Williams of Mississippi to come back into the party.

In 1972, my brother, Atlanta City Councilman James Bond, and I filed a challenge with the Credentials Committee of the Democratic National Convention against the Georgia delegates elected under a Carter-constructed system. We charged racial and sexual discrimination in the make-up of the Carter-led delegation. We won the challenge, and the compromise that resulted provided fair representation for Georgia voters.

When New York City teetered on the brink of bankruptcy, former Governor Carter opposed federal aid, but now says he only opposed federal aid to the city that would by-pass state government. And now he also says he favors by-passing the states in distributing revenue-sharing funds. Jimmy Carter blames "New York bosses" for challenges that were filed against his delegate slates, but neglects to add that he himself challenged slates in New York State.

Carter's strongest black supporter, U.S. Rep. Andrew Young of Atlanta's Fifth District [see "Why I Support Jimmy Carter" by Representative Young, *The Nation*, April 3, reprinted on pages 213-219 of this publication] says that Jimmy Carter wants to drive bosses like Mayor Richard Daley out of the party, but Carter instructs his Illinois delegates to vote for Daley, to insure Daley the chairmanship of the Illinois delegation. Carter says that when he becomes President he's going to fire Agriculture Secretary Earl Butz, but that sounds like an echo of Richard Nixon's cheap promise to fire then-U.S. Atty. Gen. Ramsey Clark, and it echoes the boastful claim of every candidate that he will hire his own men.

Carter vacillated on the issues after his New Hampshire primary victory, but responded to queries about his chameleon-like campaign rhetoric by saying, "These attacks don't hurt me — they hurt America." Sound familiar? Carter tells a questioner who seeks full information about changes he proposes in the nation's foreign policy, "I'll discuss that in my inaugural address."

Carter says he has never benefited from federal crop subsidies, but now Department of Agriculture officials say he did. When Jimmy Carter visited Europe while preparing for his campaigns, he indicated that his appointments were made by the Coca-Cola Company, not by State Department officials.

Jimmy Carter has had undeniable success in putting together a dream coalition of blacks and anti-black voters, of working class whites and businessmen, and thus appears to be a tempting candidate — to those voters who hold victory higher than principle. In North Carolina and in Florida, his success with black voters can be attributed to his brave posture as the Wallace slayer. In Massachusetts and in Illinois, he can thank the ineptitude of the opposition.

Southern Baptists are fond of saying that "prayer changes things." Jimmy Carter's religiosity has certainly had that effect on him, in fact has changed him from Left to Right to Center so many times that converts to the Carter cause ought to take a cue from an earlier apostle — Thomas, who doubted.

Liberal voters who are long tired of losing election battles may want to lay down their liberalism and convert to Carter. I'll stick with Morris Udall of Arizona. □

A Cleveland Ward Turns to Carter, But Commitment Seems Lukewarm

WILLIAM K. STEVENS
Special to The New York Times

CLEVELAND—Joe Mazzeo is a tall stringbean of a plumber who lives with his wife and children upstairs over St. Rocco's Parish Cedit Union in the middle of Cleveland's West-side Fifth Ward, in the house where he was born 48 years ago. He is also Ward Five's Democratic leader, a man who is listened to in matters political.

The other night, though, the immediate objects of Mr. Mazzeo's attention were the 10 pins at the end of a bowling alley at Brookgate Lanes in one of the city's southwestern suburbs. He rolled his first practice ball: Crash. A strike. "Nothin' to it," he grinned, puffing on a cigar, spreading his arms for emphasis, palms upward.

Almost as easily as that, Ward Five in the last six weeks appears to have become Jimmy Carter country — up to a point. "I think he's a winner," Mr. Mazzeo said between bowling turns the other night.

Mr. Mazzeo said he believed that Ward Five was the former Georgia Governor's for the taking in the Ohio Democratic Presidential primary on June 8. Since the ward is traditionally and faithfully Democratic, that makes Mr. Carter its new favorite in Presidential politics. On the ward's past form, Mr. Carter would be a sure winner here in November as well.

Lukewarm Commitments

Talks with individual voters and Cleveland politics-watchers suggest that Mr. Mazzeo's assessment is right. If it is, that represents a startling shift in sentiment since mid-March — from almost total fragmentation of opinion to something approaching consensus — in this urban, industrial enclave where 22,000 people live, typically, in modest frame houses on neatly trimmed lots in neighborhoods where there seems to be a church on one corner and a bar on the next.

But if Mr. Carter has surged into the favorite's role in the ward, it does not necessarily mean he has stirred men's souls or turned them into fervent believers. His support may have broadened dramatically, but it sometimes seems to lack depth and commitment; to be lukewarm, as if there were no other really good choice.

"I'm not too crazy about any of 'em." Tony Vannello said of the candidates the other night between frames at the bowling alley. "About a year ago my man was Wallace, and I changed to Carter. I'm not really sure why."

Mr. Vannello, a 33-year-old friend of Mr. Mazzeo's who sells and services carpets for a living, was one of a small group who gather at Brookgate Lanes once a week to bowl, drink, cuss and talk until well after midnight.

Some of the men live in the Fifth Ward; others, like Mr. Vannello, have moved from there to the suburbs, and they have thereby extended the ward's political mentality outward while retaining strong ties to the ward itself.

"It's important to beat Ford," Mr. Vannello said, "We have to have a Democrat in to pick things up. I voted for Nixon and it was a big mistake. Everything went up. Prices, everything.

"I guess you have to go with the one who can win," he said of his decision to favor Mr. Carter. "The only way a candidate can prove how good a President he would be is to get elected."

Such, perhaps, has been one effect on some rank-and-file Democrats. They, too, want a winner. Mr. Mazzeo says he thinks that the simple fact of the Carter

---

This is another in a series of articles on voter attitudes in four American communities — urban, small-city, suburban and rural — that will appear from time to time during the 1976 campaign.

---

momentum is mainly what accounts for the Georgian's surge here. Apart from that, voters' explanations as to why they favor Mr. Carter often come up vague.

"I just like the way he talks," said Kenny Jablonski, another of the bowlers who said he favored Mr. Carter. "It's the smile, maybe."

Even Mr. Mazzeo, who has been an often-lonely Carter supporter since the first soundings of sentiment were made here nearly 12 weeks ago, has difficulty explaining it. "I just took to him," he says. "It might be his sincerity — how he's talking to the people."

Ward Five is a richly various urban territory stretching across the city's near West Side from the edge of Cleveland's downtown core to the industrial flats, where the rising and falling smokebillows of the Jones & Laughlin Steel Company symbolize the industrial economy on which the jobs of most of the ward's breadwinners depend.

Its ethnic mixture of Italian, German, Irish, Polish, Ukrainian, Czech, Appalachian Mountain and Puerto Rican heritages make it a classic melting pot. Its

The New York Times/Larry Rubenstein

Joe Mazzeo, Ward Five's Democratic leader, after bowling a strike recently. "I think he's a winner," Mr. Mazzeo said of Jimmy Carter between frames.

Democratic political heritage has not wavered in any recent election.

Even in 1972, when many of the ward's voters expressed increasingly conservative learnings, broke away from the Democratic Party and voted for Richard M. Nixon, Senator George McGovern still won the ward by 247 votes out of 5,867 cast.

When the first 1976 soundings of opinion were made here during the deep-winter days of February before the first primaries, ward residents were found to be basically distrustful of government, concerned primarily about making a living, deeply resentful toward people with power and money.

In retrospect it was an attitude made to order for Governor Carter, and Mr. Mazzeo said then that he favored Mr. Carter. But he seemed nearly alone, and no other candidate seemed to have attracted much interest either. Governor Wallace was the only exception.

Support Not Unanimous

Now, as spring turns the neighborhood's streets green and leafy, Mr. Carter's emergency seems apparent. Support for him is hardly universal, however. Some diehard Wallace feeling remains, for example. And a young woman, who said she favored Representative Morris K. Udall, also said she had "certain vibes" about Mr. Carter: negative vibes having to do with what is widely perceived as his tendency to come down on all sides of an issue.

Furthermore, there appears to be no real enthusiasm for Presidential politics generally, despite the shift in sentiment. There is political enthusiam, yes. It appeared at the bowling alley the other night, where

Mr. Mazzeo was asking for help in the campaign being waged for Congress by his cousin, 30-year-old Michael Climaco, formerly a Fifth Ward Councilman.

"Gimme four signs," Kenny Jablonski told Mr. Mazzeo as the bowling match got under way.

The energy at the moment is going into local politics, the close-to-home kind that involves nuts-and-bolts help for the neighborhood. "I'm more concerned with Climaco," says Mr. Mazzeo. "The Presidency is too far away." He says he will talk Mr. Carter up between now and June 8, but that is clearly secondary.

Carter's Attempt as an 'Issues Candidate'

Rowland Evans and Robert Novak

SACRAMENTO — After two successive Tuesdays of suddenly unimpressive primary election performances, Jimmy Carter has fumbled his latest effort to transform himself from a candidate of faith and love to a candidate of issues.

Carter tried last week, following disappointing results in Michigan and Maryland, to incorporate issues into his basic campaign speech; he simply could not bring it off. His delivery of one written speech was a fiasco. Moreover, Carter was on the defensive about assorted matters ranging from his religious beliefs to

INSIDE REPORT by Rowland Evans and Robert Novak. Courtesy of Field Newspaper Syndicate, 25 May 1976.

the Calley affair. Overall, neither Carter's campaign style nor voter reaction to it reflected a candidate with the Democratic presidential nomination wrapped up.

Indeed, the nomination still seems all but assured for Carter, who would be a heavy favorite in November. Nevertheless, Carter aides are troubled by stubborn voter resistance to truly accepting him as the next President. The tense mood as the Carter campaign travelled through Oregon, Nevada and California last week resulted from less than successful efforts attempting to break down that resistance.

Actually, fitful efforts to bring Carter's Campaign to a new level go back to April 6 after his narrow Wisconsin victory. Carter was advised that he must now enter a new phase with more specific discussion of issues. Nothing much happened, however — partly because of Carter's continued string of primary election wins.

But when the Carter high command met in Detroit the night of May 18, the consensus was that something must be done. Besides losing more votes, the more he campaigned in Maryland, audiences generally seemed bored by Carter. A new speech, oriented to issues was overdue.

That task was assigned to Patrick Anderson, a respected Washington author who became Carter's newest speech-writer following the kiss-and-tell defection of Robert Shrum. Anderson, though a dedicated liberal, is a Carter true-believer who will not repeat Shrum's public protests over Carter's insufficient zeal opposing black lung disease and the B-1 bomber.

After flying to Oregon from Detroit May 19, Carter delivered Anderson's new formulation. It was ingenious, if a bit disingenuous. Although Carter did not become frontrunner by discussing issues, he told audiences in Portland and Eugene that key issues "have tied me together with the voters" in "an intimate, unbreakable relationship." Specifically, he listed governmental reorganization, tax reform, welfare reform and abolition of nuclear armaments. As usual, Carter did not venture into the likes of the economy or U.S.-Soviet relations.

Carter, seemingly uncomfortable with his new package, quickly began shedding parts of it. In Las Vegas the next morning, hard by the Nevada Nuclear Test Center, Carter dropped point four banning atomic arms (though he reaffirmed his stand in answering a question). By the time he addressed a $125-a-plate dinner in Beverly Hills, Calif., that night, he was down to one issue — governmental reorganization. That well-heeled audience did not hear Carter's usual indictment of the U.S. tax system as "a disgrace to the human race."

Earlier the same day in Sacramento, Carter's speech to the state senate — packed with potential supporters resentful about Gov. Edmund G. Brown's campaign — was perhaps his worst of the year. The decision to have Carter read Pat Anderson's speech, defending government's role in an implicit attack on Brown, was admittedly ill-advised.

For the probable nominee, Carter was extraordinarily defensive. Concluding a friendly meeting with Los Angeles Jewish community leaders, Carter volunteered that he had been told of "a great deal of concern" among Jews "about my beliefs" as a Southern Baptist. He assured them he believed in "the same God that you worship" and that they should have no concern.

Earlier that day in Nevada, Carter awoke to find a front-page column in the Las Vegas Sun by Editor Hank Greenspun attacking his alleged 1971 support for Lt. William Calley and urging voters to question Carter about it at a rally that morning. When nobody asked, Carter denied Greenspun's charges and denounced Calley as a murderer. Since as governor of Georgia he in fact issued statements defending Calley, Carter was dealing in something less than the whole truth.

Such continuous rehashing of the past and obvious struggling to change his format may partially explain why Carter generates limited enthusiasm from surprisingly small crowds. It also may be a clue to why Carter, alarmed by Brown's Oregon write-in campaign, cancelled a cherished rest back in Georgia for three days of Oregon campaigning.

Jimmy Carter remains a remarkable platform performer. Abandoning serious efforts to discuss issues, Carter held his Beverly Hills audience, well-fortified by hours of drinking, entranced with talk about faith and love identical to what he said in small-town Iowa living rooms last January. What troubles some advisers is whether this talent can propel him all the way to the presidency. Given his inability to broaden his approach, it may have to be enough.

Carter's Campaign

Jimmy Carter deserves to be considered as a serious candidate for the Democratic presidential nomination, and quite possibly as the next President of the United States.

Reprinted by permission of *The Atlanta Constitution*, ©1976 (4 March, 1976).

The strong showing by the former Georgia governor in early caucus states and in the New Hampshire and the Vermont primaries and even the solid fourth he ran in Massachusetts earned him the right to be considered seriously in any case. But beyond that his record of competence, integrity and achievement can certainly bear comparison with the records of other Democratic hopefuls currently seeking the presidential nomination.

This is not intended as a formal endorsement of Carter's candidacy. Georgia has a presidential primary in early May, and it is likely that at that point the competition for the Democratic nomination will be clearer. Some presently active candidates will no longer be in the running; rumors persist that other Democrats may yet enter the late primaries. The situation may appear very different in only two months time.

This is a time, however, when it is perhaps appropriate to comment on Carter's remarkable campaign to date, and on his public record. The critical Florida primary, considered a make-or-break state for the Georgian, is next Tuesday. Moreover, the near-hysterical attacks on Carter by some national media people and some of the other candidates invite comment. Some critics seemingly hold it against Carter that he is a Southerner and that he is not part of the Washington political establishment.

This newspaper did not support Carter when he was elected governor in 1970. His principal opponent, former Gov. Carl Sanders, had been a competent and progressive governor in the 1960s and in the newspaper's view deserved an endorsement term. But there is this initial and significant thing to say about Carter's four years as governor. His administration was scandal-free, without a hint of corruption! Not even Carter's political enemies suggest that he or anyone in his administration was guilty of any crookedness in government, an important note perhaps in this era of Watergate blues and general disillusion about government.

Here then are some general comments about specific items relating to Carter and his record and his present campaign for the White House.

CAMPAIGN TACTICS. Carter has been criticized for praising Alabama Gov. George Wallace in the 1970 election in an effort to win support from Wallace admirers. Carter is more or less guilty as charged on this one. Wallace had carried Georgia in the 1968 presidential election, two years before the 1970 Georgia's governor's race. Carter attacked his opponent, Sanders, for once blocking a Wallace speech in Georgia and without doubt persuaded a number of Wallace boosters that he, Carter, was one of them. He also sought black voters' support, however, and did not use any stand-in-the-schoolhouse-door rhetoric.

CARTER AS SEGREGATIONIST. This one is a bum rap, though some of Carter's critics have tried to use the 1970 campaign as evidence. Atlanta and Georgia produced much of the black civil rights leadership for the nation in the 1950s and the 1960s. One of those leaders, Atlanta Congressman Andrew Young, is campaigning actively in Carter's behalf. The Rev. Martin Luther King Sr. is also a supporter and had this to say in an endorsement statement: "And to talk about his (Carter's) being a racist! Why, the man put jobs in the hands of the blacks. He cooperated in every way possible for the blacks of this state, as well as for everybody else. He's no part of a racist. Not a word of it could ever be true. Now I know this and I say it boldly. A good man is being knifed for no good reason and I'm here to tell you that it's not going to stop him. We're going to take it and move forward."

REORGANIZATION. The restructuring of state government was Carter's main single program while governor. And he succeeded in battling for legislative approval. There is no question that this restructuring streamlined many of the processes of government and in many ways improved the deliverance of services. How much money did it save? This question is tougher. The reorganization itself meant such substantial change in state government that it is a little like comparing apples and oranges to talk about what present costs of state government would be if the old structures still existed. But it is clear for instance that a centralization of a state computer system does mean a solid saving of money in the long run. Two specific changes in the handling of state money brought about by Carter while governor do offer rather dramatic evidence of cash savings.

1) Carter began a study after taking office of how available state funds were deposited in banks over the state. Only a few years earlier, the typical practice had been to deposit such funds in banks in non-interest drawing accounts, often as favors to bankers who had supported the winning candidate for governor. This had changed by the time Carter took office, but it was still true that those state funds usually drew very minimal interest. Carter reorganized a state depository board, studied the state's cash flow and literally offered the available state money up for bids to any Georgia bank interested in having such deposits. This as a matter of record boosted the state's income from such accounts by millions of dollars per year. In addition, Carter vastly improved the efficiency of investing such

funds. When he took office, only a bare 50.5 per cent of available state cash was drawing any interest at all. Carter boosted that figure to nearly 85 per cent in his second year in office, a percentage that continued throughout his term.

2) Carter moved during his reorganization of government to abolish the bond issuing powers of several state authorities issuing state bonds, won approval of state constitutional amendment to permit general obligation bonds, thus lifting the state's bond rating from Double-A to Triple-A. The practical effect was simply to save the state money by reducing the interest Georgia taxpayers had to pay on such state-backed bonds.

There are other things to be said about Carter's term as governor. He took a keen interest in environmental concerns, to the point of vetoing the Sprewell Bluff dam on Georgia's beautiful Flint River, one of the few governors in the country ever to buck the Army Corps of Engineers on such a project. The January 1976 issue of *Judicature*, the Journal of the American Judicature Society, has an article on the efforts made during Carter's term to modernize Georgia courts and gives Carter substantial credit for leading and supporting these efforts, observing that during his term, "Georgia courts dealt with political realities and took their first important steps toward modernization. Reformers and students in other states may learn from it."

The main thing perhaps to be said about James Earl Carter's public record in Georgia at this stage in a national campaign is simply that his record can be examined in detail and it bears scrutiny. He was an honest, competent, innovative chief executive of a large state and he filled those responsibilities with distinction. Those are credentials that at the least put him in the same league as the other candidates presently seeking the Democratic presidential nomination.

Who IS Jimmy Carter?
TOM TIEDE

There was a time when Lester Maddox thought well of Jimmy Carter. And apparently vice versa. They were competitors for Georgia's 1966 Democratic gubernatorial nomination, but not hence adversaries — with Maddox recalling the peanut farmer as "a nice fellow." And in 1970 they were cozy enough to team up on the same statehouse ticket, headed by Carter, both men traveling the stump saying kind and laudatory things about each other.

Then, shortly after Carter moved into the governor's mansion, he passed the word that his political relationship with Maddox was merely a marriage of convenience. "He started saying he was friendly to me only to win the election," Maddox says. "He started to talk about me behind my back. One day he called me into his office and told me right out that if I ever opposed him on any issue, he'd fight me with the full government resources of the state of Georgia."

So it is that Lester Maddox became perhaps the fiercest public enemy of the man who is now thought by some to be the leading Democratic candidate for the Presidency. "He's two-faced," says Maddox of Carter, "he's the biggest phony I've ever known, and I just hope to God the American people find it out before it's too late."

The accusation is not easy to digest. The quiet Georgia gentleman, a "born-again Christian" as he says it without discomfort, seems the antithesis of deceit. Yet even allowing for the customary exaggerations of the eccentric Maddox, a brief review of Carter's four years

Reprinted by permission of Newspaper Enterprise Association, 10 February 1976.

as Georgia governor hints of evidence that his idea of leadership can be at odds with fidelity and even democracy.

Some of Maddox's charges are thin. He says as governor that Carter would "lie openly" about such matters as the number of people who attended his inaugural address, multiplying the real figures (4,000 to 5,000) by as much as two. Aside from this fluff, Maddox makes a good case for the argument that Carter ran a "redneck" campaign when it served him, and waxed enlightenment when the course became more profitable.

So far as his leadership was concerned, Maddox remembers Carter as being "expensive and contrary." He says Carter's reorganization of state government (he consolidated 300 agencies into 22) cost the state "some $300 to $400 million." He says Carter added more $20,000-and-above executives to government in his four years "than were named in the entire previous history of the state." He says Carter instituted an early retirement "bribe" for judges which doubled their pensions if they accepted — "all so he could appoint his friends to the vacancies."

Though no doubt colored, Maddox's accusations are not inventions. The idea that Carter is a political opportunist with dictatorial tendencies is widely shared in Georgia. Another bitter critic, in fact, is one-time Carter supporter Tom Murphy, presently speaker of the Georgia House. Murphy says he backed Carter in 1966 and again in 1970, "but I had to give up when it became clear he just isn't the fellow he says he is. He's fooled a whole lot of people that way."

As governor, says Murphy, Carter "tried to run the state the same way he once commanded a Navy submarine — his way or else. He never asked for any advice, any suggestions, he just gave orders. Consequently, his relationship with the legislature was very bad." So bad, reportedly, that Carter once tried to steal the power from the Georgia Senate to appoint its committee chairmen. Maddox, as president of the Senate then, and the man who eventually blocked the grab, says the incident "exposed Carter once and for all for what he is, whatever that is, and I admit I don't really know what in heck he is."

Actually, few in the nation know what the heck Jimmy Carter is. Perhaps the best we can hope to know is what he has been: good man or bad.

Born again or not, there are no seraphs running for President.

Mr. Carter's Origins

BY TOM WICKER

In a conversation with reporters aboard his campaign plane the other night, Jimmy Carter talked about his political origins in a way that may tell us something about where the nation may be heading if he is elected President.

"When I ran for governor [of Georgia] in 1966 and 1970," he said, as recorded by James T. Wooten of *The New York Times*, "I told people that conservatism did not mean racism. But if I had gone in and said, 'All of you are wrong. You shouldn't have done what you did.

I'm better than you are' . . . I wouldn't have been elected. I wouldn't have gotten more than 10 percent of the votes.

"The point I'm making is that the South, including Georgia, has moved forward primarily because it hasn't been put into the position of having to renounce itself. You've got to give people credit for the progress they make and the changes in their attitudes. . . ."

It was easy, Mr. Carter said, for people to say in hindsight that there never should have been a war in Vietnam or racial discrimination in the South. But at one time, he pointed out, Congress, the Supreme Court and every state (he might have added most Presidents) accepted racial segregation. The implication was that most Americans at one time had accepted the Vietnam War, too — and that neither they nor the South could be asked to renounce themselves.

That's quite different from, say, George McGovern's "Come home, America" theme of 1972. Mr. McGovern actually meant to say that American purposes in the world had been perverted; but he was heard by many Americans to be saying, "All of you were wrong on the Vietnam war. I'm better than you are. Renounce yourselves."

■

Mr. Carter's message, in contrast, has been that "what we need is a government as good as our people" — coupled with a promise to provide such a government. This concedes past errors and misdeeds without demanding that people renounce themselves, and it reflects a political understanding that comes naturally to a Southern politician of modern times.

In a massive new book, *The Transformation of*

Southern Politics, to be published by Basic Books next September, Jack Bass and Walter De Vries tell, for instance, of a black state representative in Georgia who said of a white representative who had used the race issue in a campaign: "I know that when we close the door and get in a smoke-filled room that we can count on him. And I also know that he's got to win for us to [benefit]. And so I understand that."

In discussing Georgia politics of recent years, Bass and De Vries argue that the golden Republican opportunity of the mid-sixties failed because the party remained "narrowly conservative in ideology and country club in image" and its major candidates "failed to make even symbolic moves to attract blacks or liberals." But they see Mr. Carter and other Democrats as symbolizing "the consensus politics that dominates the contemporary Georgia Democratic Party," which retains one-party dominance.

"The Democratic coalition," they write, "consists of blacks, courthouse Democrats who have learned the benefits of black allegiance to the Democratic Party, a developing role for organized labor, rural whites with a Democratic heritage who remain suspicious of urban Republicans and their country club image, a few white urban liberals, and the top echelon of the business and financial community. . . . The self-interest of the business elite merges with blacks and working-class whites in the broad quest for modernization and economic development."

In The Nation

The Carter campaign so far resembles an effort to build something like that consensus outside Georgia. And while Mr. Carter may not be aiming literally at "one-party dominance" of the whole country, a victory for him in the November election does raise that possibility.

Every Republican national election victory since Dwight Eisenhower has been heavily aided by the Southern states. Every projection of a conservative national majority relies on the idea of a solidly conservative Republican South. The rise of Jimmy Carter, also based on Southern support, not only threatens Republican prospects in the South for 1976 but also the idea of a conservative Republican South in the future.

Mr. Carter's Southern victories over George Wallace symbolize the political fact — a new, moderate consensus of whites and blacks, business elites and the working class, replacing racism, law-and-order conservatism and the old economic exploitation. If Jimmy Carter can make that consensus hold in the South, he and the national Democratic Party will have left Republicans almost no place to go.

SUPPORT IN THE SPRING 1976 PRESIDENTIAL PRIMARIES

REPUBLICAN　　　　　　　DEMOCRATIC

Total Delegates	FORD	REAGAN	Uncommitted	To Be Chosen		Total Delegates	BROWN	CARTER	CHURCH	JACKSON	UDALL	WALLACE	Other	Uncommitted	To Be Chosen
37		37			Alabama	35		3				27		5	
19	17		2		Alaska	10								10	
27	1	26	2		Arizona	25		5			19	1			
27	10	17			Arkansas	26		17			1	5		3	
167		167			California	280	204	67	7		2				
31		3		28	Colorado	35	1	1	1		2			2	28
35				35	Connecticut	51		17		5	15			14	
17				17	Delaware	12									12
66	43	23			Florida	81		34		21		26			
48		48			Georgia	50		50							
19	4		15		Hawaii	17					1	1		15	
21	5	16			Idaho	16		2	14						
101	72	11	13	5	Illinois	169		60			3		92	14	
54	9	45			Indiana	75		51			10			14	
36				36	Iowa	47		20			12	2		13	
34	28	4	2		Kansas	34		15			2			17	
37	19	18			Kentucky	46		37			2	7			
41		36	5		Louisiana	41		13				9		19	
20	15	4	1		Maine	20	1	10			6		1	2	
43	43				Maryland	53		32		10	7			4	
43	28	15			Massachusetts	104		16		30	21	21	16		
84	57	27			Michigan	133		69			58	2		4	
42	15	5	4	18	Minnesota	65							49	16	
30	2	6	22		Mississippi	24		5	1			11	3	4	
49	15	12	3	19	Missouri	71		28		1	3		1	21	
20				20	Montana	17		4	11					2	
25	7	18			Nebraska	23		8	15						
18	5	13			Nevada	11	6	3	1					1	
21	18	3			New Hampshire	17		15			2				
67	67				New Jersey	108		25			3			75	5
21				21	New Mexico	18		8			6			4	
154	119	19	16		New York	274		33		103	73			65	
54	25	28	1		North Carolina	61		36				25			
18				18	North Dakota	13									13

These are the latest delegate standings, based on a survey by *Post* reporters and including yesterday's primary results. Yesterday's New Jersey results are incomplete. The "Others" column in the Democratic tally includes: Stevenson 86; Humphrey 54; Byrd 29; Shapp 19; Harris 15; Shriver 11; Bentsen and Stokes, 6 each; McCormack 3; Walker 2; Bayh and Muskie, 1 each. It takes 1130 votes for the GOP nomination; 1505 for the Democratic.

Post Chart by Mike DeNonno

REPUBLICAN · DEMOCRATIC

Total Delegates	FORD	REAGAN	Uncommitted	To Be Chosen	State	Total Delegates	BROWN	CARTER	CHURCH	JACKSON	UDALL	WALLACE	Other	Uncommitted	To Be Chosen
97	91	6			Ohio	152		128			18		6		
36	36				Oklahoma	37		12					7	18	
30	16	14			Oregon	34	9	11	14						
103	88	6	9		Pennsylvania	178		68		23	20	2	19	46	
19	19				Rhode Island	22		7	6					9	
36	4	26	6		South Carolina	31		11	1			8	1	10	
20	9	11			South Dakota	17		9			7			1	
43	21	22			Tennessee	46		36				1		9	
100		96		4	Texas	130		92					6		32
20				20	Utah	18									18
18	18				Vermont	12	2	3			3			4	
51	6	35	10		Virginia	54		23			7			24	
38				38	Washington	53				32	7			14	
28			28		West Virginia	33							29	4	
45	45				Wisconsin	68		25		7	25	10	1		
17	2	10	5		Wyoming	10	1	1			1			7	
—					Canal Zone	3								3	
—					Democrats Abroad	3	¹⁄₂							2¹⁄₂	
14	14				District of Columbia	17		8			5			4	
4	1		3		Guam	3								3	
8	8				Puerto Rico	22				15				7	
4			4		Virgin Islands	3								3	
2259	**966**	**863**	**151**	**279**	**Totals**	**3008**	**224**	**1118**	**71**	**248**	**328**	**168**	**233**	**492½**	**125**

These are the latest delegate standings, based on a survey by *Post* reporters and including yesterday's primary results. Yesterday's New Jersey results are incomplete. The "Others" column in the Democratic tally includes: Stevenson 86; Humphrey 54; Byrd 29; Shapp 19; Harris 15; Shriver 11; Bentsen and Stokes, 6 each; McCormack 3; Walker 2; Bayh and Muskie, 1 each. It takes 1130 votes for the GOP nomination; 1505 for the Democratic.

Post Chart by Mike DeNonno

Footnotes

COUNTRY BOY

[1] Clyde Haberman, "The Raising of Jimmy," *New York Post*, 21 May 1976.

[2] Jimmy Carter, *Why Not The Best?* (Nashville: Broadman Press, 1975), p. 22.

[3] Ibid., p. 14.

[4] Transcript from television interview on "Bill Moyers' Journal," PBS broadcast on 6 May 1976 (WETA, Washington, D.C.; WNET, New York), p. 9.

[5] Carter, *Why Not The Best?* pp. 16-17.

[6] Ibid., p. 37.

[7] Ibid., p. 35.

[8] Ibid., p. 17.

[9] B. J. Phillips, "New Day A'Coming in the South," *Time*, 31 May 1971, p. 15.

[10] Carter, *Why Not The Best?* p. 35.

[11] Ibid., p. 31.

[12] Transcript of Bill Moyers interview, p. 39.

JIMMY AND THE ADMIRAL

[1] Carter, *Why Not The Best?* p. 42.

[2] Ibid., p. 43.

[3] Ibid., p. 47.

[4] Transcript of Bill Moyers interview, p. 30.

[5] *The Lucky Bag*, U.S. Naval Academy Yearbook, 1947.

[6] Kandy Stroud, "Rosalynn Carter: Capturing Votes and Captivating Voters with her Mint Julep Voice," *Washington Star*, 14 March 1976.

[7] Carter, *Why Not The Best?* p. 53.

[8] Sally Quinn, "Behind the Grin of the Peanut Farmer from Georgia," *Washington Post*, 28 March 1976.

[9] Carter, *Why Not The Best?* p. 59.

[10] David Nordan, "Grin and Peanuts Won't Win Race," *Atlanta Journal*, 8 February 1976.

[11] Carter, *Why Not The Best?* p. 57.

[12] Transcript of Bill Moyers interview, pp. 5-6.

[13] Carter, *Why Not The Best?* p. 57.

[14] Peter Goldman and Eleanor Clift, "Carter on the Rise," *Newsweek*, 8 March 1976, p. 24.

[15] Jack Spalding, "Carter Candidacy," *Atlanta Journal*, 26 November 1974.

[16] "Who IS Jimmy Carter?" Newspaper Enterprise Association, 10 February 1976.

[17] Carter, *Why Not The Best?* p. 60.

[18] Transcript of Bill Moyers interview, p. 4.

[19] Transcript of Bill Moyers interview, pp. 4-5.

POLITICKING IN A SINFUL WORLD

[1] Carter, *Why Not The Best?* pp. 81-82. There were 80,000 citizens in the 14th senate district of Georgia.

[2] Neil Maxwell, "In 50's, Carter was ahead of pack," *Wall Street Journal*, 25 March 1976.

[3] Ibid.

[4] Carter, *Why Not The Best?* p. 97.

[5] Carter also admits that "I was so unknown that some journalists labeled me: 'Jimmy Who?' " in his autobiography. *Why Not The Best?* p. 98.

[6] Bruce Galphin, "Jimmy Carter — A New Breed," *Atlanta Constitution*, 2 July 1966.

[7] Ibid.

[8] Ibid.

[9] Carter, *Why Not The Best?* p. 98.

REDNECK JIMMY VS. CUFFLINKS CARL

[1] Carter, *Why Not The Best?* p. 100.

[2] Reg Murphy and Hal Gulliver, *The Southern Strategy* (New York: Charles Scribner's Sons, 1971), p. 176.

[3] Bill Shipp, "Carter Turned Right to Triumph," *Atlanta Constitution*, 8 November 1970.

[4] Bill Shipp, "The Carter Package Was a Breeze to Sell," *Atlanta Constitution*, 11 November 1970.

[5] Carter, *Why Not The Best?* pp. 102, 103.

[6]   Bill Shipp, "Carter Turned Right to Triumph."

[7]   Murphy and Gulliver, *The Southern Strategy*, p. 189.

[8]   Carter, *Why Not The Best?* p. 101.

[9]   Murphy and Gulliver, *The Southern Strategy*, pp. 186-87.

[10]   Steven Brill, "Jimmy Carter's Pathetic Lies," *Harper's Magazine*, March 1976, pp. 77-78.

[11]   Quoted from an interview with Charles Kirbo.

[12]   " Carter Juggles Old South and New," *Atlanta Journal*, 26 August 1971.

[13]   Bill Shipp, "The Carter Package Was A Breeze to Sell."

[14]   Ibid.

[15]   Ibid.

[16]   Interview with Leroy Johnson, *Atlanta Constitution*, 7 January 1971.

[17]   Murphy and Gulliver, *The Southern Strategy*, pp. 193-94.

[18]   Quoted from an interview with Ben Fortson.

[19]   George Lardner, Jr. "Jimmy Carter — *Promises, Promises*," *Washington Post*, 7 March 1976.

[20]   Ibid.

SOUTH GEORGIA TURTLE FOR GOVERNOR

[1]   Charles Mohr, "Carter Credibility Issue — Calley and Vietnam War," *New York Times*, 20 May 1976.

[2] Bill Shipp, *Atlanta Constitution*, 16 April 1971.

[3] Goldman and Clift, "Carter on the Rise," *Newsweek*, 8 March 1976, p. 29.

[4] James T. Wooten, "Carter's Record as Georgia's Governor: Activism and Controversial Programs," *New York Times*, 17 May 1976, pp. 1, 22.

[5] T. McN. Simpson, "Georgia State Administration: Jimmy Carter's Contribution," paper delivered at the 1973 annual meeting of the Southern Political Science Association, Knoxville, Tennessee.

[6] For an expansion of Julian Bond's characterization of Carter and Carter's record, see "Why I Don't Support Jimmy Carter," reprinted on pages 220-223 of this publication.

[7] Howell Raines coins this phrase in "Carter Chips Liberal Image," *Atlanta Constitution*, 17 September 1973.

A NEW VOICE FROM THE SOUTH

[1] B. J. Phillips, "New Day A'Coming in the South."

[2] Murphy and Gulliver, *The Southern Strategy*, pp. 196-97.

[3] "Carter Juggles Old South and New."

[4] Don Oberdorfer, "Carter: Ready Grin, Homespun Manner," *Washington Post*, 16 January 1976.

[5] Jules Witcover, "Carter Sought the Number 2 Spot on McGovern Ticket," *Washington Post*, 23 April 1976.

[6] Elizabeth Drew, "A Reporter in Washington D.C. (Journal III)," *New Yorker*, 31 May 1976.

[7]   Carter, *Why Not The Best?* p. 137.

[8]   Eleanor Clift, "Prophetic Game Plan," *Newsweek*, 10 May 1976, pp. 28-29.

[9]   Carter, *Why Not The Best?* p. 141.

[10]   Eleanor Clift, "Prophetic Game Plan," pp. 28-29.

[11]   Allen Ehrenhalt, "Carter Campaign Raises 'Issue' Issue," *Congressional Quarterly*, 1976.

[12]   Carter, *Why Not The Best?* p. 141.

RUNNING FOR WHAT?

[1]   Reg Murphy, "Jimmy Carter's Running for WHAT?" *Atlanta Constitution*, 10 June 1974.

[2]   Jack Spalding, "Carter Candidacy."

[3]   Eleanor Clift, "Prophetic Game Plan," p. 29.

[4]   Carter, *Why Not The Best?* pp. 141, 142.

[5]   Robert Walters, "Putting the Carter Before the Horses," *National Journal*, 29 November 1975.

[6]   Michael Novak, "The Hidden Religious Majority," *Washington Post*, 4 April 1976.

[7]   David S. Broder, "Carter: Love Is Sweeping the Nation," *Washington Post*, 18 January 1976.

[8]   Richard Reeves, "Carter's Secret," *New York Magazine*, 22 March 1976.

[9]   "Old Values," *Time*, 23 February 1976, p. 13.

[10]   CBS-*New York Times* surveys/interviews. *New York Times*, 25 February 1976. This and succeeding notes to the *New York Times* refer to results of CBS-*New York*

Times Surveys made under the general supervision of Professor Carey Orren of the Government Department of Harvard University; interviews were conducted by George Fine of Research, Inc., of New York.

[11] CBS-*New York Times* surveys/interviews. *New York Times*, 10 March 1976.

[12] CBS-*New York Times* surveys/interviews. *New York Times*, 17 March 1976.

[13] Steven Brill, "Jimmy Carter's Pathetic Lies," p. 88.

[14] Jack Germond, "Attack on Carter by Liberals Fierce," *Washington Star*, 4 February 1976.

[15] Ibid.

[16] Ibid.

[17] Ibid.

[18] William Raspberry, "The Mystery of Carter's Support Among Blacks," *Washington Post*, 28 May 1976.

[19] Richard Cohen, "Blessing of the Pastor: Strong Endorsement," *Washington Post*, 6 May 1976.

[20] Interview with Sam Roberts, *New York Sunday News*, 4 April 1976.

[21] CBS-*New York Times* surveys/interviews. *New York Times*, 7 April 1976.

[22] Ibid.

[23] CBS-*New York Times* surveys/interviews. *New York Times*, 28 April 1976.

[24] Ibid.

[25] CBS-*New York Times* surveys/interviews. *New York Times*, 19 May 1976.

[26] CBS-*New York Times* surveys/interviews. *New York Times*, 9 June 1976.

BORN AGAIN

[1]　Garry Wills, "The Plains Truth,"*Atlantic Monthly*, June 1976, p. 54.

[2]　Transcript of Bill Moyers interview, pp. 12-13.

[3]　Transcript of Bill Moyers interview, p. 12.

[4]　Sally Quinn, "Behind the Grin of the Peanut Farmer from Georgia."

[5]　E. Brooks Holified, "The Man's Religion," *New Republic*, 5 June 1976, p. 15.

[6]　Transcript of Bill Moyers interview, p. 28.

[7]　Carter, *Why Not The Best?* p. 129.

[8]　Transcript of Bill Moyers interview, p. 6.

[9]　E. Brooks Holified, "The Man's Religion," p. 16.

[10]　Transcript of Bill Moyers interview, p. 32.

[11]　"Jimmy Carter's Big Breakthrough," *Time*, 10 May 1976, p. 16.

[12]　Hunter S. Thompson, "Fear and Loathing on the Campaign Trail, Third-Rate Romance, Low-Rent Rendezvous," *Rolling Stone*, 3 June 1976, p. 88

[13]　Garry Wills, "The Plains Truth," pp. 53-54.

[14]　E. Brooks Holified, "The Man's Religion," p. 16.

[15]　Michael Novak, "The Hidden Religious Majority."

[16]　George F. Will, "The Spirit That Moves Jimmy Carter," *Washington Post*, 1 April 1976.

[17]　Transcript of Bill Moyers interview, p. 33.

[18]　Transcript of Bill Moyers interview, p. 7.

[19]　Morris B. Abrams, "Carter and Baptists," *New York Times*, 4 June 1976.

[20]   Quoted in James Reston's "Carter, Evangelism, and Jews," *New York Times*, 6 June 1976.

[21]   William Lee Miller, "Singing with Brenda, Carl, Shirley — And Jimmy," *Washington Post*, 17 May 1976.

[22]   Hal Gulliver, "Carter Politics in a Sinful World," *Atlanta Constitution*, 6 May 1976.

[23]   Carter, *Why Not The Best?* p. 116.

[24]   Transcript of Bill Moyers interview, p. 35.

THE PRIVATE MAN

[1]   Myra McPherson, "Carter's Biggest Booster," *Washington Post*, 24 May 1976.

[2]   Sally Quinn, "Behind the Grin of the Peanut Farmer from Georgia."

[3]   James T. Wooten, "The well-planned enigma of Jimmy Carter," *New York Times Magazine*, 6 June 1976, p. 78.

[4]   Transcript of Bill Moyers interview, p. 11.

[5]   Carter, *Why Not The Best?* p. 120.

[6]   Sally Quinn, "Behind the Grin of the Peanut Farmer from Georgia."

[7]   Ibid.

[8]   Ibid.

[9]   Hunter S. Thompson, "Fear and Loathing on the Campaign Trail, Third-Rate Romance, Low-Rent Rendezvous," p. 88.

[10]   Ibid., p. 87.

[11]   James T. Wooten, "The well-planned enigma of Jimmy Carter," p. 16.

[12]   Transcript of Bill Moyers interview, pp. 33-34.

[13]   James T. Wooten, "Carter's Record as Georgia's Governor: Activism and Controversial Programs."

[14]   Transcript of Bill Moyers interview, p. 11.

[15]   Carter, *Why Not The Best?* p. 72.

[16]   Goldman and Clift, "Carter on the Rise," p. 26.

[17]   Kandy Stroud, "Rosalynn Carter: Capturing Votes and Captivating Voters with her Mint Julep Voice."

[18]   Ibid.

[19]   Ibid.

[20]   Ibid.

[21]   Karen Elliot House, "Jimmy Carter's Wife Speaks Softly and Shares His Ambitious Drive," *Wall Street Journal*, 17 June 1976.

[22]   Ibid.

[23]   Myra McPherson, "Carter's Biggest Booster."

[24]   Ibid.

[25]   Karen Elliot House, "Jimmy Carter's Wife Speaks Softly and Shares His Ambitious Drive."

[26]   Myra McPherson, "Carter's Biggest Booster."

[27]   Ibid.

[28]   Ibid.

A CARTER PRESIDENCY

[1]   James T. Wooten, "Carter, Tired But Happy, Chats About Hopes, Plans, Roots, Faith," *New York Times*, 16 June 1976.

[2] David Nordan, "Grin and Peanuts Won't Win the Race."

[3] Transcript of Bill Moyers interview, p. 19.

[4] Albert R. Hunt, "Jimmy Carter's Advisers," *Wall Street Journal*, 25 May 1976.

[5] Ibid.

[6] Ibid.

[7] Robert Walters, "The Boys on the Carter Bus," *National Journal*, 29 May 1976.

[8] Ibid.

[9] David S. Broder, "The Oregon Primary: A Pause for Reflection?" *Washington Post*, 26 May 1976.

[10] Ibid.

[11] Albert R. Hunt, "Jimmy Carter's Advisers."

[12] Steven Brill, "Jimmy Carter's Pathetic Lies," p. 88.

[13] Transcript of Bill Moyers interview, p. 15.

[14] C. Vann Woodward, *The Burden of Southern History* (Baton Rouge: Louisiana State University Press, 1968). The four characteristics are discussed at length in the chapter entitled "The Search for Southern Identity."

[15] James T. Wooten, "Excerpts from Conversation with Jimmy Carter," *New York Times*, 16 June 1976.

[16] Charles Mohr, "Carter Credibility Issue — Calley and Vietnam War."

[17] James T. Wooten, "Excerpts from Conversation with Jimmy Carter."

[18] Address by Governor Jimmy Carter to the Chicago Council on Foreign Relations (Atlanta: Jimmy Carter Presidential Campaign, 15 March 1976), p. 3.

[19]   Transcript of Bill Moyers interview, p. 26.

[20]   Ibid., pp. 26, 27.

[21]   James T. Wooten, "Excerpts from Conversation with Jimmy Carter."

[22]   Ibid.

APPENDIX

[1]   "Jimmy Carter Presidential Campaign Issues Reference Book," 15 March 1976, p. 15.

[2]   Ibid., p. 14.

[3]   Ibid., p. 18.

[4]   News Release by Jimmy Carter on Consumer Affairs (Atlanta: Jimmy Carter Presidential Campaign, 1976), p. 2.

[5]   "Interview on the Issues — What Carter Believes," *U.S. News & World Report*, 24 May 1976, p. 18.

[6]   "Jimmy Carter Presidential Campaign Issues Reference Book," p. 22.

[7]   Ibid., p. 25.

[8]   Ibid., p. 10.

[9]   Ibid., p. 20.

[10]   Hobart Rowan, "Carving an Economic Platform," *Washington Post*, 1 April 1976.

[11]   "Jimmy Carter Presidential Campaign Issues Reference Book," p. 19.

Bibliography

Publications:

Abrams, Morris B. "Carter and the Baptists." *New York Times*, 4 June 1976.

Brill, Steven. "Jimmy Carter's Pathetic Lies." *Harper's Magazine*, March 1976, pp. 78-88.

Broder, David S. "Carter: Love Is Sweeping the Nation." *Washington Post*, 18 January 1976.

Broder, David S. "The Oregon Primary: A Pause for Reflection?" *Washington Post*, 26 May 1976.

Carter, Jimmy. Address by Governor Jimmy Carter to the Chicago Council on Foreign Relations. Atlanta: Jimmy Carter Presidential Campaign, 15 March 1976.

Carter, Jimmy. News release by Jimmy Carter on Consumer Affairs Atlanta: Jimmy Carter Presidential Campaign, 1976.

Carter, Jimmy. *Why Not The Best?* Nashville: Broadman Press, 1975.

"Carter Juggles Old South and New." *Atlanta Journal*, 26 August 1971.

Clift, Eleanor. "Prophetic Game Plan." *Newsweek*, 10 May 1976, pp. 28, 29.

Cohen, Richard. "Blessing of the Pastor: Strong Endorsement." *Washington Post*, 6 May 1976, pp. B-1, B-5.

Drew, Elizabeth. "A Reporter in Washington, D.C. (Journal III)." *New Yorker*, 31 May 1976, pp. 54-56, 58, 63, 64, 66, 68-70, 71, 74-76, 78-99.

Ehrenhalt, Allen. "Carter Campaign Raises 'Issue' Issue." *Congressional Quarterly*, 1976.

Galphin, Bruce. "Jimmy Carter — A New Breed." *Atlanta Constitution*, 2 July 1966.

Germond, Jack. "Attack on Carter by Liberals Fierce." *Washington Post*, 6 May 1976, p. A-3.

Goldman, Peter and Clift, Eleanor. "Carter on the Rise." *Newsweek*, 8 March 1976, pp. 24-30.

Gulliver, Hal. "Carter Politics in a Sinful World." *Atlanta Constitution*, 6 May 1976.

Haberman, Clyde. "The Raising of Jimmy." *New York Post*, 21 May 1976, p. 19.

Holified, E. Brooks. "The Man's Religion." *New Republic*, 5 June 1976, pp. 15-17.

House, Karen Elliot. "Jimmy Carter's Wife Speaks Softly and Shares His Ambitious Drive." *Wall Street Journal*, 17 June 1976.

Hunt, Albert R. "Jimmy Carter's Advisers." *Wall Street Journal*, 25 May 1976.

"Interview on the Issues — What Carter Believes." *U.S. News and World Report*, 24 May 1976, p. 18, 19, 23.

"Jimmy Carter Presidential Campaign Issues Reference Book," 15 March 1976.

"Jimmy Carter's Big Breakthrough." *Time*, 10 May 1976, pp. 11, 16-24.

Lardner, George Jr. "Jimmy Carter — *Promises, Promises*." *Washington Post*, 7 March 1976.

The Lucky Bag. U.S. Naval Academy Yearbook. 1947.

Maxwell, Neil. "In 50's, Carter was ahead of pack." *Wall Street Journal*, 25 March 1976, pp. C-2, C-3.

McPherson, Myra. "Carter's Biggest Booster." *Washington Post*, 24 May 1976, pp. A-1, A-5.

Miller, William Lee. "Singing with Brenda, Carl, Shirley — And Jimmy." *Washington Post*, 17 May 1976, p. A-21.

Mohr, Charles. "Carter Credibility Issue — Calley and Vietnam War." *New York Times*, 20 May 1976.

Murphy, Reg. "Jimmy Carter's Running for WHAT?" *Atlanta Constitution*, 10 June 1974.

Murphy, Reg and Gulliver, Hal. *The Southern Strategy*. New York: Charles Scribner's Sons, 1971.

Nordan, David. "Grin and Peanuts Won't Win Race." *Atlanta Journal*, 8 February 1976.

Novak, Michael. "The Hidden Religious Majority." *Washington Post*, 4 April 1976.

Oberdorfer, Don. "Carter: Ready Grin, Homespun Manner." *Washington Post*, 16 January 1976.

"Old Values." *Time*, 23 February 1976, p. 13.

Phillips, B. J. "New Day A'Coming in the South." *Time*, 31 May 1971, pp. 14-20.

Quinn, Sally. "Behind the Grin of the Peanut Farmer

from Georgia." *Washington Post*, 28 March 1976.

Raines, Howell. "Carter Chips Liberal Image." *Atlanta Constitution*, 17 September 1973.

Raspberry, William. "The Mystery of Carter's Support Among Blacks." *Washington Post*, 28 May 1976.

Reeves, Richard. "Carter's Secret." *New York Magazine*, 22 March 1976.

Reston, James. "Carter, Evangelism, and Jews." *New York Times*, 6 June 1976.

Rowan, Hobart. "Carving an Economic Platform." *Washington Post*, 12 April 1976.

Shipp, Bill. "The Carter Package Was a Breeze to Sell." *Atlanta Constitution*, 11 November 1970.

Shipp, Bill. "Carter Turned Right to Triumph." *Atlanta Constitution*, 8 November 1970, p. 2-A.

Shipp, Bill. *Atlanta Constitution*, 16 April 1971.

Simpson, T. McN. "Georgia State Administration: Jimmy Carter's Contribution." Paper delivered at the 1973 annual meeting of the Southern Political Science Association, Knoxville, Tennessee, pp. 1-33.

Spalding, Jack. "Carter Candidacy." *Atlanta Journal*, 26 November 1974.

Stroud, Kandy. "Rosalynn Carter: Capturing Votes and Captivating Voters with her Mint Julep Voice." *Washington Star*, 14 March 1976.

Thompson, Hunter S. "Fear and Loathing on the Campaign Trail, Third-Rate Romance, Low-Rent Rendezvous." *Rolling Stone*, 3 June 1976, pp. 52-55, 58-64, 84, 87-88.

Tiede, Tom. "Who IS Jimmy Carter?" Newspaper Enterprise Association, 10 February 1976.

Walters, Robert. "The Boys on the Carter Bus." *National Journal*, 29 May 1976.

Walters, Robert. "Putting the Carter Before the Horses." *National Journal*, 29 November 1975.

Will, George F. "The Spirit That Moves Jimmy Carter." *Washington Post*, 1 April 1976.

Wills, Garry. "The Plains Truth." *Atlantic Monthly*, June 1976, pp. 49-54.

Witcover, Jules. "Carter Sought the Number 2 Spot on McGovern Ticket." *Washington Post*, 23 April 1976.

Woodward, C. Vann. *The Burden of Southern History*. Baton Rouge: Louisiana State University Press, 1968.

Wooten, James T. "Carter, Tired But Happy, Chats About Hopes, Plans, Roots, Faith." *New York Times*, 16 June 1976, pp. 1, 19.

Wooten, James T. "Carter's Record as Georgia's Governor: Activism and Controversial Programs." *New York Times*, 17 May 1976, pp. 1, 22.

Wooten, James T. "Excerpts from Conversation with Jimmy Carter." *New York Times*, 16 June 1976, p. 18.

Wooten, James T. "The well-planned enigma of Jimmy Carter." *New York Times Magazine*, 6 June 1976, pp. 16, 17, 76, 78, 80, 82, 86-89.

Interviews:

CBS-*New York Times*, surveys made under the general supervision of Professor Carey Orren of the Government Department of Harvard University, and interviews conducted by George Fine of Research, Inc., of New York. *New York Times*. 25 February 1976, 10 March 1976, 17 March 1976, 7 April 1976, 28 April 1976, 19 May 1976, 9 June 1976.

Carter, Lillian, quoted from an interview with.

Fortson, Ben, quoted from an interview with.

Gulliver, Hal, quoted from an interview with.

Johnson, Leroy, interview with. *Atlanta Constitution*. 7 January 1971.

Kirbo, Charles, quoted from an interview with.

Moyers, Bill. Transcript from television interview on "Bill Moyers' Journal." PBS broadcast. WETA, Washington, D.C.; WNET, New York; 6 May 1976, pp. 4-7, 9, 12, 13, 28, 30, 32, 33, 35, 39.

Roberts, Sam, interview with. *New York Sunday News*. 4 April 1976.

Shipp, Bill, quoted from an interview with.

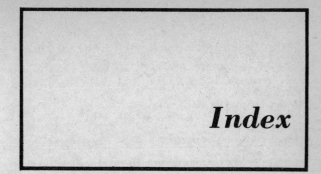

Index

DATE DUE

SE 23 '80			
NO 24 '80			
DE 1 '80			
NO 19 '81			
DE 6 '82			
MAR 1 7 '89			
GAYLORD			PRINTED IN U.S.A